# Young Savers Rule(s)

# Young Savers Rule(s)

TAX-FREE SNOWBALL MAGIC

• • •

*Meade Greenberg & Tom Guignon*

**Disclaimer: Very Important**

This guide is provided for general information only, and nothing contained in the material constitutes a recommendation for the purchase or sale of any investment. The statements of fact in this book are obtained from sources that the authors deem to be reliable. The views expressed in this guide are based on research materials available from sources considered reliable. Views are subject to change on the basis of additional or new research, new facts, or developments.

The investment risks described herein are not purported to be exhaustive, and any person considering an investment should seek independent advice on the suitability or otherwise of the particular investment. The reader understands that it is his or her responsibility to seek legal and/or tax advice regarding legal and tax consequences of his or her transactions.

This guide is copyrighted material. Any unauthorized duplication is prohibited.

Copyright 2016 Meade Greenberg & Tom Guignon

All rights reserved.

ISBN: 1539368483
ISBN 13: 9781539368489
Library of Congress Control Number: 2016917471
CreateSpace Independent Publishing Platform
North Charleston, South Carolina

# Table of Contents

Introduction: To Whom Have You
Been Listening? · · · · · · · · · · · · · · · · · · · · · · · · · · vii

Chapter 1  Do You Know What Financial Road You're On? · · · 1
Chapter 2  Why Tax-Free? · · · · · · · · · · · · · · · · · · · · · · · 7
Chapter 3  Taking a Closer Look at Retirement Savings · · · · · 25
Chapter 4  Understanding Retirement Distribution Triggers · · · 39
Chapter 5  Life Insurance—The Ultimate Tax-Free
Planning Vehicle · · · · · · · · · · · · · · · · · · · · · · · 44
Chapter 6  Saving for College Using Tax-Free Strategies · · · · · 54
Chapter 7  Affluent Millennials · · · · · · · · · · · · · · · · · · · · 63
Chapter 8  Inheriting Tax-Deferred and Tax-Free Assets · · · · · 76
Chapter 9  Retirement Certainty with the Check-a-Month
Plan · · · · · · · · · · · · · · · · · · · · · · · · · · · · · · · 80

Summary / Rules for Young Savers · · · · · · · · · · · · 85
Resources · · · · · · · · · · · · · · · · · · · · · · · · · · · · 87
About the Authors · · · · · · · · · · · · · · · · · · · · · · 91

# Introduction: To Whom Have You Been Listening?

• • •

AS AMERICANS, WE OPERATE UNDER a very basic assumption: we should work, be law-abiding citizens, and pay our taxes. In exchange, the government will provide the services that individuals cannot, such as federal defense, road maintenance, fire and police departments, and public school systems. Our government also performs thousands of other visible and invisible tasks as a result of this social contract.

As we march through life, we also know that we should save some money, invest for the future, and hopefully create a nice nest egg that will allow us to live comfortably in retirement and possibly even pass on something to our children.

It all sounds so lovely, doesn't it?

Unfortunately, there is a big problem with this picture. Basically, it isn't really panning out for most people, and young people especially are being set up for a harsh wake-up call when they near retirement. The root of the issue is that the US tax system has become so convoluted, confusing, and bureaucratic that nobody's dreams are being fulfilled. That nest egg that we're saving or planning to save? We don't get to keep all of it. In fact, much of that money will someday belong to the government.

There are ways to plan so that you keep more of your own money, but they require breaking from the way that things have "always been done." It means that you must take charge of your money and your future by learning about your options.

## Why this book is different

You might be surprised at yourself for having picked up this book. Reading about financial literacy doesn't exactly sound like a fun, light read, but it is so fantastic that this book is in your hands. The amount of money you will have in the future depends on it.

What it comes down to is this: you can bury your head in the sand and cross your fingers and toes in hopes that your money accumulates, or you can face your financial situation and make choices right now that will help build your wealth, provide for your family, and ensure that when you retire, you'll be able to enjoy yourself.

There is a whole financial world out there that you may know nothing about. That's what we will teach you about in this book. The way that young people today should be planning for their financial futures is different than the way things have always been done. In fact for many of us, doing things the conventional way can be downright detrimental.

The advice in this book comes from two different viewpoints. One is the perspective of Tom, a forty-plus-year veteran of the financial services industry who has been involved in market ups and downs and is extremely comfortable with all facets of investing and financial planning. Tom has spent his life learning about the different financial products available and making them work to his clients'—not the government's—benefit.

The other viewpoint comes from his daughter Meade, who, while in the same boat that many other young investors are in today, has the advantage of a lifelong education in what works and what doesn't. Meade knows that many people her age have barely started planning for their financial future or are having a hard enough time with day-to-day expenses and aren't sure where to even begin when it comes to saving and retirement.

It might sound daunting, but by learning a little bit about the tax code and options for saving, investing, and retirement, you can make a huge difference in your financial future. And the sooner you start, the better, because the less you know about taxes, the more you'll likely end up paying. This book will show you how to avoid that trap and end up with more money in your savings and investment accounts and therefore in your control.

And why can't you just get this information from your average financial advisor or bank? Because it's quite likely that they cannot or will not give advice about tax-free alternatives. Some financial advisors want to help you grow your money; however, they will refrain from giving any kind of tax advice. The problem is that without this kind of advice, you could be setting yourself up to owe as much as *half* of your entire wealth to the government. That being said, there are good financial advisors who will help young savers.

Essentially, this book will teach you about the "game" of financial planning and taxes, and how to make it all work for *you*. While this game is essentially unavoidable—yes, you still must pay taxes—you can play your very best hand, maximizing your money and ultimately your future.

CHAPTER 1

# Do You Know What Financial Road You're On?

• • •

THROUGHOUT OUR LIVES, MOST OF us work hard for our money. But the reality is, if you use the proper strategies, your money can work just as hard—if not harder—for you, providing you with the ideal retirement in the future.

If you've ever been involved on a sports team or even in a simple game of Monopoly, you know that getting ahead involves a bit of strategy. But it isn't always the biggest and the brawniest who come out to be the winners, nor is it always the ones who are the longtime favorites. In fact, in many cases, it simply takes knowing where you're going and why and then keying in on those goals.

The same holds true when investing for retirement. While it may seem like it's a long way off, the decisions that you make today really can make a difference. Choosing the right path today can relieve you of a great number of headaches later on.

## WHAT YOU DON'T KNOW CAN HURT YOU
It's unfortunate that many young adults are not fully prepared to deal with a lot of the financial decisions that they will face

throughout their lifetimes. Most grade schools, high schools, and even colleges today do not teach students even the basics of how a home or a car loan works, how credit cards work, or what mutual funds, 401(k) plans, or IRA accounts are.

Many young people also do not know how to open a basic checking or savings account, or why investing in tax-free options can be much more beneficial than investing in tax-deferred retirement accounts, especially over the long term.

But these are concepts that are absolutely essential for you to know, and if you master them now, you will be much better prepared going forward. Many young people today simply do not have access to the right information, primarily as it relates to taxes and their investments.

How do we know that hardworking taxpayers are not getting good tax advice? One clear indicator is that less than 5 percent of retirement assets are in tax-free retirement (for example, Roth) accounts, which we will discuss in greater detail in the coming chapters. In other words, people are simply not taking advantage of tax-free accounts that help money snowball rather than melt away.

This means that after years and years of building up a substantial amount of savings, most people are simply handing over a sizable chunk of that money to the IRS rather than keeping it all for themselves.

But there are ways that you can allow your retirement savings to grow without being taxed *and* withdraw the funds tax-free in retirement. Young people aren't being geared toward these options, but we want to change that. We're willing to bet that if more people knew about tax-free investing and the many advantages that it provides, there would be more people going that route. That's what this book is about.

## Where is your financial road leading you?

If you've been in the workforce for several years, or even if you are just getting started in your career, then it's possible that you may have some savings set aside. You might be involved in an employer-sponsored retirement plan, such as a 401(k), and possibly even have some personal funds in a brokerage fund and/or savings account.

But regardless of what you've got and how much you have set aside, the real question is, do you truly know how those accounts work and how they are working for *you*?

Politicians and bankers have created a giant mess with tax laws and borrowing programs that literally make it impossible to understand how to save in a clear and simple way. For example, most young people know how to get credit cards, how to get a student loan, how to get the biggest mortgage, and how to borrow more.

Today, the latest bank-debt scheme is the new deferred credit cards that "allow" you to make no payments for six months, a year, or even three years. The big banks actually encourage you to borrow, borrow, and borrow more. They charge insanely high interest rates of 7 percent on student loans and 15 percent on credit cards.

Debt, however, can absolutely crush your ability to save, and if you fall for these borrowing schemes, you run the risk of falling behind unless you attain some good financial advice along with a plan for climbing out from under it. (See Resources at the end of this book for more information on how to get out of debt.)

Everyone has his or her own unique financial goals, and only you can truly decide what yours are. What do you envision your future retirement to be like? Although it may seem eons away, the earlier you start to save for it, the easier it will be to attain your goals.

In getting started, it is also important to have a good understanding of the types of accounts that are available to you and why one may be better than another in terms of accomplishing your goals. And while you don't have to know the IRS tax code inside and out, knowing the difference between tax-free and tax-deferred retirement investing can make a world of difference. In the coming chapters, we will explain the types of tax-free accounts that are available to everyone and why they should be the primary choice for most young people today.

## What's *Really* in a Name?

What's in a name? Well, when it comes to investing and tax concepts, there's actually quite a lot. Much of it can be confusing in and of itself. But then there's the issue of similar-sounding names like "tax-deferred" and "tax-free."

Although these two names may sound extremely similar, they actually denote very different concepts. Something that is tax deferred must eventually have taxes paid on it, whereas something that is tax-free will not need to have any tax payments made whether you withdraw it now or in the future. We'll discuss many examples of these types of accounts in the coming chapters, so don't worry if you don't fully understand them now. The point is that while they sound similar, they represent two very different futures for you and your investments.

## Who are you listening to?

Where do most young people get their financial information today? Well, that depends. For most, just trying to get everything done each day can leave little time for proactive learning about money and investing.

The demands on our time these days—work, kids, social activities, hobbies—can be overwhelming, so seeking out financial advice is usually just another item at the bottom of our long to-do lists. Since it's not always easy to understand or readily available, it's no wonder that, according to a Charles Schwab survey, workers spend more time planning a vacation than they do planning for retirement.

When it comes to money matters, it seems that young people get their information from a variety of sources. These can include their employer-sponsored retirement plan (if they have one), banks and credit unions, friends and spouses, and, if they are lucky, parents and/or grandparents who have taught them the benefits of saving and investing for the future.

There are "client-first" financial planning companies that employ client-first financial advisors who will work with young savers even if they are only starting with $1,000. Maybe one of these advisors gave you this book for your journey. Work with this advisor if you can.

Even so, much of this information still encourages young people to take the tax-deferred route. What does this mean? It means that while you may not have to pay taxes on some amount of money that you decide to save today, you will *eventually* be paying taxes on it, likely when the money has substantially accumulated. Even if you are setting aside something for your future, it is well worth considering making some changes to the ways that you're saving that could put you in a much better place in a decade or two.

## How to get on the right road, or even on the road to get started

If you feel like you may need to make some adjustments to your savings—or if you just need to get a plan started—it's easier than you might think. It doesn't take much to get started, and you don't have to start with a lot.

In fact, doing something is much better than doing nothing at all. From there, much like a snowball picks up momentum, you'll be amazed at how quickly your funds can grow, especially when you aren't required to pay taxes on the gains.

While the IRS and taxes will never go away, there are ways that you can strategize in your investing in order to help yourself avoid them as much as possible. All it takes is knowing the "rules" and having an understanding of the different types of accounts that you can use.

You've already taken the first step toward tax-free financial planning by learning about the potential financial roads for you. In the following chapters, we'll tell you exactly how and why you should make minor adjustments in the way you save that will have major implications on your future.

CHAPTER 2

# Why Tax-Free?

• • •

TAXES. THEY ARE THE SECOND certainty in life, along with death—and yes, we will also be discussing life insurance later in the book. So it's important that you understand the basics of taxes as they relate to you. Seeing the beauty of tax-free planning is only possible if you understand how our system works.

Unfortunately, understanding our tax system is no easy task, and sitting down to do your taxes tends to get more complicated as you get older. This is usually because you make more money, have more investments, get married, have kids, own a business, or have some combination of any or all of the above. You name it, it can complicate your taxes.

That's why many people end up turning to an expert or, at the very least, to some type of online "system" to help wade through their tax returns each year. If this includes you, that's OK. We actually recommend utilizing a service that offers either partial or complete assistance with your taxes.

With that in mind, it is still important for you to know how the tax code works in order to take the proper steps in planning your future finances in an intelligent way.

As we walk you through the big ideas, you might also find your eyes glazing over and drool creeping out of the side of your mouth, but hang in there. It really won't be that bad. In fact, once you realize how the system works and how much more of your own money you can actually be keeping—and growing—for yourself by doing things a certain way, you might even find it interesting, beneficial, and fun. And once you see the hard numbers, we think you'll find it to be extremely rewarding.

## Tax-free versus taxable Income

When doing your taxes, knowing what to claim as taxable and nontaxable income can make a big difference in your overall tax liability. Your income can be acquired in a number of different ways, such as wages, interest, tips, and commissions. In most cases, money that you earn is likely going to be taxable, at least to some extent. In fact, there is very little that is nontaxable during your working years.

However, what you do with that money in terms of investing it after it's been earned can literally make a world of difference in your lifetime, and we will show you just how much of a difference throughout this chapter.

The way in which taxes are (or aren't) applied to an investment can also make an incredible difference in the end result, especially over a long period of time. We will provide you with some concrete examples of the difference between taxable versus tax-free income in this chapter in order to show you just how much of a difference tax-free can offer, even over tax-deferred types of accounts, which is something that many financial advisors today still preach.

## How tax brackets really can affect the rate at which money gets taxed

The most basic thing that you will need to understand about the tax code in order to help yourself pay less in taxes—and to essentially keep more of your own money in your pocket—is tax brackets.

These brackets come to you and all of us in the good old US of A thanks to the Internal Revenue Service, better known as the IRS. While some politicians would like to argue that they can "eliminate" the IRS, that is simply not going to happen—at least not any time soon.

Although resented by many, the IRS is a necessary component of the functioning of our government.

So, after accepting its existence, it is important that you understand the basics of the tax system in order to properly plan and navigate your financial future. To make things easier, we will walk you through the basics without getting too complicated in the process.

For starters, these four IRS tax tables refer to the four different ways that you can file your taxes. You determine which of these you belong in based upon your marital status. Then, your income will determine your tax bracket.

| Chart #1: IRS Tax Tables | | | |
|---|---|---|---|
| Single | Married Filing Jointly | Married Filing Separately | Head of a Household |

Depending on the actual amount of your income, you will fall into one of seven different tax brackets. Knowing your individual tax bracket is the first step to understanding what percentage of your money you must give the government in terms of your earnings.

So, in looking at these examples, using 2015 figures, the lowest tax bracket for single people requires that you earn $9,225 or less. If you fall into this category, then you will owe 10 percent of that income to Uncle Sam. But if you earn any more than that amount, not every single dollar that you earn may be taxed at the very same percentage.

For instance, single tax filers pay (in 2015) the following tax rates on income:

**Chart 2: Single Taxpayer 2015 Chart**

| Taxable Income | Tax Rate |
| --- | --- |
| $0 to $9,225 | 10% |
| $9,226 to $37,450 | $922.50 plus 15% of the amount over $9,225 |
| $37,451 to $90,750 | $5,156.25 plus 25% of the amount over $37,450 |
| $90,751 to $189,300 | $18,481.25 plus 28% of the amount over $90,750 |
| $189,301 to $411,500 | $46,075.25 plus 33% of the amount over $189,300 |
| $411,501 to $413,200 | $119,401.25 plus 35% of the amount over $411,500 |
| $413,201 or more | $119,996.25 plus 39.6% of the amount over $413,200 |

Source: IRS.gov

Using an example, let's say that you actually earn just $100 more than $9,225, or a total of $9,325. In that case, you would owe 10 percent tax on the money that falls into the first bracket. So you would owe 10 percent on the first $9,225 that you earned (10% × $9,225 = $922.50 in tax).

But then you would also owe 15 percent on that $100 amount that spilled over into the next bracket. Income in the next bracket is taxed at 15 percent. Therefore, the additional $100 that you earned would be taxed at 15 percent, so you would owe $15 on those earnings ($100 × 15% = $15 in tax). In total for the year, your taxes would be $937.50 ($922.50 + $15 = $937.50).

This method is applied for any income amount. The key is to remember that out of your entire income, different segments of your money are taxed at different rates. It's easy to see that as you make more money, you pay more in taxes.

Let's imagine an individual has an income of $100,000. This level of income falls into the 28 percent tax bracket. But that does not mean that he or she will pay 28 percent of $100,000 (or $28,000 in total income taxes). In fact, the person's tax bill is actually just over $21,000. Here's why: money that falls into each tax bracket is taxed at a different rate. The chart below represents the individual's total income of $100,000. The money falls into four different brackets, and the amount in that range is taxed at whatever rate corresponds to that particular bracket.

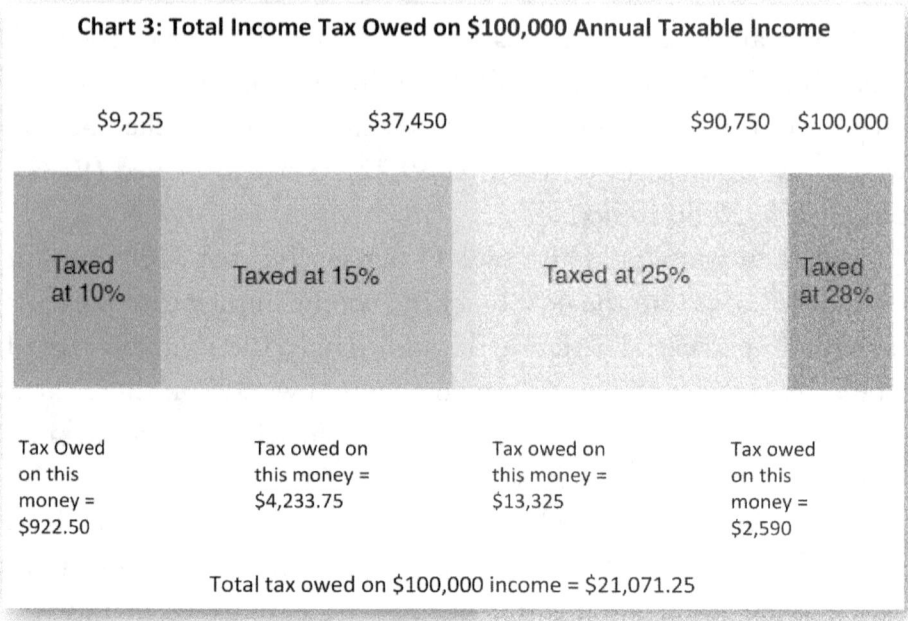

And the tax brackets keep going. For example, if you were to add $50,000 more income to $100,000, that amount will be taxed at 28 percent, or $14,000.

So here is a question to consider. Do the rich *always* pay more in taxes? The answer is, not necessarily. In fact, Warren Buffett, one of the wealthiest men on the planet, has made the statement that his secretary pays a higher *percentage* of income tax than he does.

Why is that?

Let's look at an example, which makes several assumptions, including the following:

- She is unmarried, so she files as a single taxpayer.
- Her annual taxable income is $37,450.

Using the table above, we can see that Mr. Buffett's secretary will pay tax of 10 percent on the first $9,225 of her income. So she will owe $922.50 and will also owe 15 percent on the remainder of her income up to the $37,450. So, since $37,450 - $9,225 = $28,225, she will pay 15 percent tax on $28,225. This tax will be $4,233.75. Therefore, her total tax bill will be $922.50 + $4,233.75, which equals $5,156.25.

Now let's take this example a step further and imagine that she also holds a taxable bond as an investment and that she earns $1,000 in interest on that bond. Because that interest is counted as taxable income, it will spill into the next tax bracket. Any amount of income that is over $37,450 will be taxed at a rate of 25 percent. So her tax on that $1,000 in interest will be $250 ($1,000 × 25%).

If her income from wages was *more* than $37,450, it is possible that her tax bill on that interest from her bond would be even more. This is because as income gets higher, the income tax rates goes up to 28 percent, 33 percent, 35 percent, and even 39.6 percent. So if that bond had spilled her into a higher bracket, that money would be taxed at a higher rate. Brackets matter.

However, it is obvious that Warren Buffett makes much more than $37,450 per year. So what exactly does he mean when he says that he pays a lower tax rate than his secretary?

Well, he means that even though he technically earns a great deal more, he pays a lower *percentage* on the money he earns. Mr. Buffett earns his money primarily through capital gains, or returns on his investments in stocks or other assets that are considered capital assets in which he has invested his money.

Capital gains are not taxed according to the regular income tax schedule, and they are not included in "income" when calculating your income tax. In fact, capital gains have their own tax schedule, which is actually quite a bit lower in most cases. Depending on a taxpayer's level of income, capital gains are taxed at either 15 percent or 20 percent.

Therefore, in Warren Buffett's case, he is only taxed at a rate of 20 percent on most of his income because most of his income comes from capital gains instead of wages, whereas his secretary pays 25 percent or 28 percent—or more, as we assume she makes more than $37,450 per year—on her income.

Now we can also assume that, due to the massive amount of capital gains that Warren Buffett typically earns each year, he is usually hit with a substantial tax bill in terms of the dollar amount, but the percentage is lower than his secretary's tax bracket. And, as Mr. Buffett has pointed out many times, this just does not seem fair.

In addition to the lower tax brackets for capital gains versus income, there are also other loopholes that can allow the wealthy to keep more of their money. For example, hedge funds have what is referred to as "carried interest." This is taxed at a lower rate than most brackets.

Various tricks like these are legal, and they allow wealthy people—who you would assume are taxed at the highest rate of 39.6 percent on all their income—to pay a much lower rate on a lot of the money that they bring home. The important takeaway is to know that everyone is playing the game. Mr. Buffett, for example, is playing the ultimate tax-free game. Although it's not a fair game, if you learn the rules, you can play too.

For instance, take a look at lines 8a and 8b from the IRS 1040 tax form below. These are very important, and what you put in them can substantially change how much you owe the government. Line 8a represents taxable interest, which is taxed at whatever rate you fall into in the tax schedule. Line 8b is for tax-exempt interest. You do not pay *any* taxes on this kind of interest.

| Income | 7 Wages, salaries, tips, etc. Attach Form(s) W-2 | 7 | |
|---|---|---|---|
| | 8a Taxable interest. Attach Schedule B if required | 8a | |
| | b Tax-exempt interest. Do not include on line 8a . . . | 8b | | |

How does this affect taxes? It can have a bigger impact than you might think. So again, let's take a look at an example. This time we'll use a married couple filing jointly, with a joint taxable income of $74,900.

At this income amount, the couple will owe the government $10,312.50. That tax amount is determined by taking 10 percent of their income, up to $18,450, and then 15 percent of the rest of their total income.

Let's imagine that the couple then earned an additional $10,000 in taxable interest from their investments. Since this bumps them into the next tax bracket, they would pay 25 percent tax on that amount to the government.

So their total tax bill for the year would be $12,812.50 ($10,312.50 from their income + $2,500 from their taxable interest = $12,812.50). However, if the interest on their investment had been tax exempt, they would owe no taxes on that $10,000 interest, and they would have saved themselves $2,500 in taxes for the year.

Having that type of tax-exempt status can become even more valuable when people fall into higher tax brackets. For instance, if the couple in our example had a joint taxable income of $465,000 and were in a tax bracket of 39.6 percent, they would have had to pay $3,960 in taxes on that $10,000 in interest. Ouch. This is exactly why everyone should be utilizing tax-free planning.

Look again at Form 1040, only this time look at lines 9a and 9b. These are somewhat similar to lines 8a and 8b, and they are important to examine as well. Line 9a refers to ordinary dividends, and line 9b refers to qualified dividends.

| Income | 7 | Wages, salaries, tips, etc. Attach Form(s) W-2 | | 7 | |
|---|---|---|---|---|---|
| | 8a | Taxable interest. Attach Schedule B if required | | 8a | |
| Attach Form(s) W-2 here. Also attach Forms | b | Tax-exempt interest. Do not include on line 8a | 8b | | |
| | 9a | Ordinary dividends. Attach Schedule B if required | | 9a | |
| | b | Qualified dividends | 9b | | |

A dividend is a sum of money that is paid regularly (usually on a quarterly basis) by a company to its shareholders. Qualified dividends have a lower tax rate (15–20 percent) than ordinary dividends.

However, there are certain requirements that must be met for dividends to be classified as qualified. For example, the stock must be issued by a US-based corporation, and the stock must be held for a certain length of time. Ordinary dividends, however, are just exactly that—ordinary. These types of dividends are counted as regular income, and they are subject to the same tax schedule too.

So if we go back to the example of the married couple with the taxable income of $74,900, we can see that an additional $10,000 of ordinary dividends would be taxed at 25 percent. If, however, those dividends were instead considered qualified dividends, they would only be taxed at a rate of 15 percent.

Qualified dividends are taxed at most at 20 percent, and that is only for the highest tax-bracket earners, those who are in the 39.6 percent bracket. So, in this regard, it is obvious why wealthy people with high incomes would want as much of their money as possible to come from qualified dividends and to be taxed at 20 percent instead of 39.6 percent.

Chart 4: Example of Taxable Interest, Dividend, and Capital Gain on $10,000

| | Amount Taxed | Amount Taxed | Net Spendable | Net Spendable |
|---|---|---|---|---|
| Additional income classified as: | 25% Bracket | 39.6% Bracket | 25% Bracket | 39.6% Bracket |
| Taxable Interest $10,000 | $2,500 | $3,960 | $7,500 | $6,040 |
| Ordinary Dividends $10,000 | $2,500 | $3,960 | $7,500 | $6,040 |
| Qualified Dividends $10,000 | $1,500 | $2,000 | $8,500 | $8,000 |
| Capital Gain $10,000 | $2,000 | $2,000 | $8,000 | $8,000 |
| Tax-free Interest $10,000 | $0 | $0 | $10,000 | $10,000 |

Clearly, the $10,000 of tax-exempt (tax-free) interest is the perfect choice.

For a married couples filing jointly (as well as for any qualifying widow/er) in 2015, the tax rates are as follows:

### Chart #5: Married Couple Filing Jointly

| Taxable Income | Tax Rate |
|---|---|
| $0 to $18,450 | 10% |
| $18,451 to $74,900 | $1,845.00 plus 15% of the amount over $18,450 |
| $74,901 to $151,200 | $10,312.50 plus 25% of the amount over $74,900 |
| $151,201 to $230,450 | $29,387.50 plus 28% of the amount over $151,200 |
| $230,451 to $411,500 | $51,577.50 plus 33% of the amount over $230,450 |
| $411,501 to 464,850 | $111,324.00 plus 35% of the amount over $411,500 |
| $464,851 or more | $129,996.50 plus 39.6% of the amount over $464,850 |

Source: IRS.gov

## Tax deferral of dividends and capital gains

Now let us look at one more big fact that must be understood by young savers. Do not convert a qualified dividend (15 percent tax) or a capital gain (20 percent tax) into ordinary income taxes with a tax-deferred account. Why?

Because a tax-deferred account automatically converts qualified dividends and capital gains to ordinary income brackets. So if you are in the 28 percent tax bracket at payout time of qualified dividends and capital gains from a tax-deferred account, you magically convert a 15 percent tax to possibly a 28 percent or maybe even a 39.6 percent tax. Not good tax planning.

## It's not just about your tax bill!

It is easy to see from the chart above that the best solution is the $10,000 investment that is exempt from taxes. Your tax bill each year is less if you don't have to pay taxes on any interest or capital gains. But that's not all. If that money is parked in a tax-free account, it also grows exponentially more than if it is in a taxable account. Let's look at the snowball effect of tax-free planning.

We'll start with an example of tax-free versus taxable investing. Let's take two investors, each of whom invest $1 and assume that each year their money doubles.

Investor A is invested in a tax-free account and is therefore not required to pay any tax on her earnings. Investor B must pay 20 percent of his yearly gain to the government. Therefore, when his $1 grows to $2 in the first year, he must pay 20 percent of the $1 gain, or $0.20, in tax.

The following year, investor B has $1.80, since $0.20 went to the government, so his money doubles to $3.60. However, investor B must pay 20 percent of his gains of $1.80, or $0.36, in tax, which leaves him with only $3.24 at the beginning of the following year. Investor A had $2 in the tax-free account, her money doubled again to $4, and she wasn't required to pay any taxes on that $2 gain. The end result after twenty-five years between the tax-free and the taxable accounts is amazing.

## Chart #6: Warren Buffett Tax-Free Difference

| End of Year | Investor A: Tax-Free | Investor B: Taxable (at 20%) |
|---|---|---|
| 1 | $2.00 | $1.80 |
| 2 | $4.00 | $3.24 |
| 3 | $8.00 | $5.83 |
| 4 | $16.00 | $10.49 |
| 5 | $32.00 | $18.89 |
| 6 | $64.00 | $34.01 |
| 7 | $128.00 | $61.22 |
| 8 | $256.00 | $110.19 |
| 9 | $512.00 | $198.35 |
| 10 | $1,024.00 | $357.04 |
| 15 | $32,768.00 | $6,746.64 |
| 20 | $1,048,576 | $127,482 |
| 25 | $33,554,432 | $2,408,865 |

Here's another thing to consider. We use a 20 percent tax in this example, but what if investor B was in the 39.6 percent bracket instead? The answer is that the government would get a lot more than they got from an investor who was in the 20 percent bracket.

The tax-free compounding still gives nothing to the government. So imagine if instead of just twenty-five years, you invested your money over a period of fifty years or more.

We realize that the numbers in the above example are essentially impossible to attain. For instance, it would likely take a miracle to get a 100 percent return or even an 80 percent return on $1. And while no one invests $1 and comes out twenty-five years later with $33 million, it does illustrate the power of tax-free compounding investing.

In order to make things a bit more realistic, let's take a look at another example between the tax-free and taxable accounts, using a more representative 10 percent return with individuals who are investing $10,000 per year.

### Chart #7: $10,000 Invested Per Year

| End of Year | Tax-Free | Taxable (at 20%) |
|---|---|---|
| 5 | $67,156 | $63,359 |
| 10 | $175,311 | $156,454 |
| 15 | $349,497 | $293,242 |
| 20 | $630,021 | $494,229 |
| 25 | $1,081,817 | $789,544 |

Imagine being able to watch your tax-free account value literally snowball. Take for instance the above tax-free example. If the $1,081,817 were to remain in the account for just five additional years earning 10 percent, it would be worth nearly another $800,000, and that's with no ordinary dividend, qualified dividend, taxable interest, capital gain, and investment income tax. Zero. Nada. It truly is something to marvel at.

While the tax-free investor can simply enjoy watching that account grow, an investor who is in the 20 percent tax bracket gets hit fairly hard. And just think how much harder the hit would be if he were in a 28 percent, 33 percent, 35 percent, or 39.6 percent tax bracket. Looking at this example right now makes it appear simple and obvious, but many investors still choose taxable or tax-deferred accounts over tax-free ones.

One reason why people choose a tax-deferred account is because many old-school financial planners stress the benefits of deferring income *today*, rather than the benefits of being able to withdraw your funds tax-free *tomorrow*. This advice overlooks the fact that if your money is in a taxable account, you pay taxes on your gains, *and* taking your money out *also* affects your tax bracket.

Whatever money you withdraw from a tax-deferred retirement account would not only be taxable but could also potentially kick you into an even higher tax bracket. If your money comes from a tax-free account, you not only do not have to pay taxes on it, but it also does not affect what tax bracket you fall into.

## So how do I do *that*?

So how do you invest money that grows and is tax exempt? By putting your money into accounts that legally allow the money to accumulate without requiring taxes on your gains. Yes, these accounts exist.

There are several types of accounts that allow you to set aside money, invest it, and watch it accumulate tax-free. It's important to remember, however, that some of these accounts require you to use that money in a certain way. This is not your rent money, grocery money, or vacation money, but since you should be saving anyway, these accounts are perfect places for you to stash your cash for the future.

Over the next few chapters, we'll walk you through these accounts. Here are the ones we'll be discussing. We'll also show you how and why they are the preferred investment vehicles over traditional taxable or tax-deferred accounts.

- Retirement accounts: Traditional IRAs and 401(k)s require you to pay taxes on the money that grows in the account. Roth IRAs and Roth 401(k)s are *tax-free* when you withdraw the funds. The difference is that when you contribute money to a traditional IRA or 401(k), you can deduct that money on your taxes, saving you a bit of money up front, and you cannot deduct money contributed to Roth accounts. However, we will show you that this perceived saving through deduction is *nothing* compared to the amount of money you will save when your money comes out tax-free at the time of your retirement.
- Life insurance accounts: Money that is paid out from a life insurance account is *not taxable*. We are big advocates of parking your money in some type of life insurance. We will show you how this will be extremely beneficial to your family.
- 529 savings accounts: Do you plan on having children? Would you like to send them to college? If you open a 529 savings account, the money in the account can be invested and will grow, and you *won't have to pay taxes* on it. If you're hoping to educate your children or grandchildren anyway, why not set that money aside and let it grow *tax-free*?
- Accounts for affluent savers: If you've already utilized the above types of accounts, there are even more ways to set aside money so that it can grow without being taxed. We'll discuss some more ways to allocate your money so that you and your family have the best possible future financial health.

## The bottom line

When you start working and supporting yourself, it can be difficult to imagine that you'll ever be old. But that day will come. So ask yourself, would you rather pay taxes on a smaller amount of money now or on the amount that your money will (hopefully) grow to in the future?

When it comes to saving and investing, you have a lot of different options that are available to you, and while it may not seem all that urgent right now, the choices that you make today can and will have a significant effect on how—and how well—you will live your life down the road. This is especially the case as it pertains to taxable and tax-deferred versus tax-free accounts.

For most people who are in the workforce today, a tax-free account is by far the best type of account to have. Allowing your money to grow without the worry of having to pay taxes on the gain or on the withdrawals can literally allow your funds to expand exponentially. Building a snowball and rolling it over without taxes in the future is the ideal option. In the next few chapters, we'll show you exactly how you can maximize your financial future.

CHAPTER 3

# Taking a Closer Look at Retirement Savings

• • •

DEPENDING ON WHERE YOU ARE in your career, what your current expenses are, and the type of lifestyle that you live (for example, whether you've opted for the brand-new BMW or chosen to stick with the used Dodge Stratus for a few more years), you may or may not already be socking away money for your future retirement.

Even though retirement may seem like a long way off, it's important to do what you can, starting now, to put away funds for the future. If you can do so using a tax-free option, it typically turns out that much better in the long run, even though most financial advisors will likely steer you toward the "traditional" options that allow you to defer your contributions now versus taking the tax advantages later. But as we'll explain in this chapter, the delayed tax-free gratification can be more than worth the wait.

## A BRIEF PRIMER ON RETIREMENT SAVINGS PLANS

If you work for a corporation or a business that offers a retirement savings plan, it is likely that the plan is a 401(k). If, however, you work for a public school system or various other tax-exempt organizations, the retirement plan that you participate in may be a 403(b) instead.

In either case, you are allowed to defer a certain percentage of your earnings each year into these plans, and the funds can grow without being taxed on their gains until the time that they're withdrawn. At that time, usually at retirement, the full amount of the withdrawal will be taxed as ordinary income.

The false premise behind these types of retirement plans is that you will be in a lower tax bracket when you make these withdrawals and that therefore it helps to ease the taxable burden at least somewhat when taking your money out of the plan in retirement. But this isn't necessarily true. In fact, in many cases, people are actually in a *higher* tax bracket when they retire. So in essence this could make your tax-deferred retirement plan what we like to refer to as a "ticking tax time bomb."

Many people, in addition to having an employer-sponsored retirement plan, will also opt to open an individual retirement account, or IRA. These accounts allow you to deposit a certain amount of money each year while also letting the funds inside of the account grow without being taxed each year.

For many years there was only one type of IRA account that was available to investors. This is the version that is now known as the traditional IRA. But while the traditional IRA can offer some nice benefits, the newer Roth IRA version can provide you with many more advantages when it comes to both growing your investments and withdrawing your future income.

## Traditional versus Roth

One of the key differences between IRA accounts—as well as for retirement accounts overall—is in their tax treatment. For instance, the traditional IRA will allow you, in most cases, to make a contribution that is tax deductible. This means that the amount of money you put into the account each year can be deducted from income on your taxes. This tax deduction allows, in some cases, more dollars to be invested versus an after-tax Roth account.

The traditional IRA also allows tax-deferred growth of the funds within the account. What this means is that unlike in a regular investment account, where you would be taxed on any gains that you realized each year, the growth in your traditional IRA is not taxed until the time you withdraw the money, which could be many years in the future.

This will allow these funds to grow and compound exponentially because you are essentially earning on top of earnings, and earning on top of the money that *would have otherwise* been taxed.

But while this all sounds great and wonderful—and it can be—when the time comes to withdraw the money, many people are blindsided because they didn't realize just how much they would end up having to pay out in taxes.

Tax-deferred, then, is really just another name for putting off your taxes until a time in the future. It doesn't mean that you'll never have to pay tax on that money; rather, it means that you will need to pay it at some point down the road.

Many financial advisors may tell you that in retirement you may be in a lower tax bracket, so the funds will be subject to a lower tax rate than they would have been if payable before retirement. But that still doesn't change the fact that you'll likely be paying income tax on 100 percent of the funds that you're withdrawing from your traditional IRA.

Why on 100 percent?

It's because you were able to "defer" your traditional IRA—or 401(k) or 403(b)—contribution when it was made. So because the IRS gave you a break and didn't make you pay income tax on those funds in the year that you made the contribution, they are having you make up for it in retirement. And at that time, it is likely that you'll have a whole lot more money to be taxed.

Alternatively, you could choose to go with a Roth option instead. With this type of account, you make your contribution with money that has already been taxed. So you don't get the benefit of the income tax deferral like you do with the traditional account.

However, the Roth option more than makes up for it with its tax-free status. This is because not only is the growth on your funds inside of a Roth account not taxed, neither are your withdrawals in the future, provided that you are at least age fifty-nine and a half and the account has been open for at least five years.

Think about the difference in taxation between a traditional and a Roth account this way: would you rather put off having major surgery until some time in the future or not have to have the surgery at all because you lived a healthy lifestyle during your younger years?

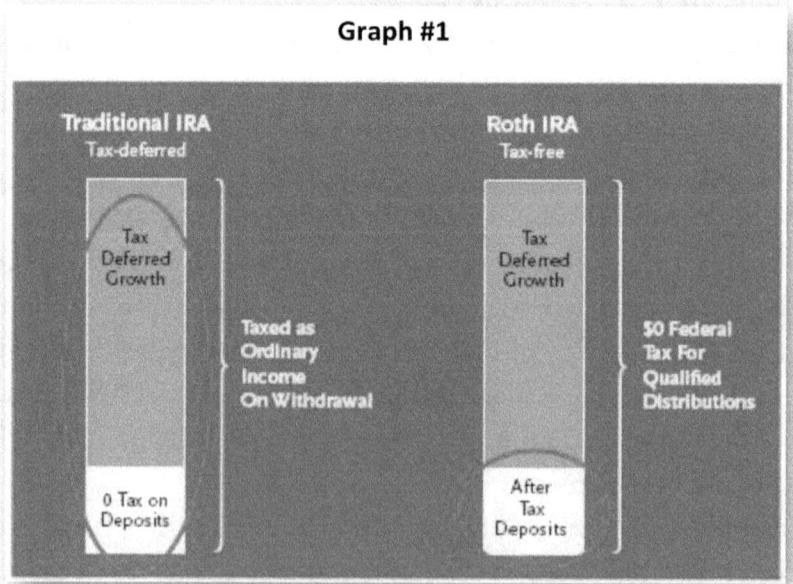

Source: Advanced Brokerage Concepts (http://abcinsfin.com/index.php/insurance101/tax-free-retirement/)

Take a look at the two accounts in the graphic above. Which one would you rather be withdrawing your money from?

It is easy to see what a difference investing in tax-free versus tax-deferred options for retirement can make. But unfortunately today, many young people are still primarily using tax-deferred savings for almost everything.

Why is that?

One reason is because that's the way it has "always been" in the past. And when we don't have any other options to choose from, it becomes difficult at best to invest your money any other way.

For example, if you work for a company that offers an employer-sponsored retirement plan such as a 401(k), take a look at your plan's information. Do you have the option of investing your money in a Roth 401(k) or 403(b) option? Chances are that the answer to that question is a resounding no.

But today, there is the option of having not only a personal Roth IRA account but also an employer-sponsored 401(k) or 403(b) plan. So, if your company does not currently offer this type of a plan, inquire how they may go about starting one.

Imagine what it would be like if every single cent in your 401(k) or 403(b) plan could be withdrawn tax-free in retirement after thirty or forty or more years of saving and growing those funds.

This could provide you with a substantial advantage over a traditional plan, where the withdrawals are currently taxed anywhere between 10 percent and 35 percent when they come out, and in the future they could possibly be taxed in excess of 42 percent, depending on your federal income tax bracket.

## Why the Roth option makes more sense

While you may not pay taxes on the contributions that go into a traditional IRA, 401(k), or 403(b) plan, there are some definite benefits that can more than make up for that by going with a Roth IRA and/or retirement plan option.

For example, one of the biggest advantages is that you will have tax-free withdrawals on your money. This can be particularly beneficial for younger investors, as there is more time to let your money grow tax-free inside of the Roth account.

Also, while both Roth and traditional accounts have annual contribution limits, technically the after-tax dollars that are placed inside of a Roth can essentially go further. This is because you will still owe tax on the money that is inside of a traditional account but not the money that is inside of the Roth.

Roth accounts can also have other benefits. For example, unlike a traditional IRA, you can withdraw the amount of your original Roth IRA contribution without being penalized even if you are under the age of fifty-nine and a half, provided that you leave the earnings inside of the account.

You are also not forced to begin making withdrawals when you turn age seventy and a half when you own a Roth, but you are with traditional IRA and 401(k) plans. In fact, if you do not start taking withdrawals from these accounts, the IRA will penalize you. Not so with a Roth. Therefore, the money that is inside of a Roth plan can continue to grow until *you* are ready to take it out, not Uncle Sam.

**Chart #8: Roth versus Traditional Retirement Accounts**

| | Traditional | Roth |
|---|---|---|
| **Maximum Annual IRA Contribution (in 2016)** | 100% of annual compensation or $5,500 (if age 49 or younger) / $6,500 (if age 50 or older), whichever is less. | Same as Traditional IRA, subject to phase-out range, depending on modified adjusted gross income. |
| **Maximum Retirement Plan Contribution (in 2016) for 401(k), 403(b), and most 457 plans** | <ul><li>$18,000 if age 49 and younger</li><li>Additional $6,000 for age 50 and older</li></ul> | <ul><li>$18,000 if age 49 and younger</li><li>Additional $6,000 for age 50 and older</li></ul> |
| **Deductible Contributions** | Yes - either fully or partially | No |
| **Federal Income Tax Treatment on Earnings** | Earnings grow tax-deferred until distributions begin. | Earnings grow tax-free. |
| **Federal Tax Treatment on Withdrawals** | Distributions are taxed as ordinary income. | Qualified distributions are tax-free. |
| **Distributions** | Distributions from contributions and earnings can be taken after age 59 1/2 without federal tax penalty. Mandatory withdrawals must begin no later than April 1 following the year the account holder reaches age 70 1/2.<br><br>**Distributions could trigger taxes on Social Security retirement benefits. Could also cause Medicare premium to cost more.** (Covered in more detail in Chapter 4). | Distributions from contributions can be made any time without taxes or tax penalty. Distributions from earnings are tax-free if the initial contribution to the account was made at least 5 years prior and the account holder meets one of the following:<ul><li>age 59 1/2</li><li>disabled</li><li>purchasing a first home (up to $10,000 lifetime maximum)</li></ul>**Distributions from a Roth IRA will not trigger taxes on Social Security retirement benefits. These distributions will also not increase Medicare premium.** |
| **Required Minimum Distributions (RMDs)** | Account holder must begin taking RMDs no later than April 1 of the year following the year he or she turns age 70 1/2. | No RMDs apply during the account holder's lifetime. Also, more tax-free is possible. (Inherited Roth - see Chapter 8). |

## Roth 401(k) and Roth 403(b)

Will you qualify for a Roth 401(k) or Roth 403(b) retirement account? Yes. However, your employer must offer a Roth option so you can participate. Should all employers make a Roth 401(k) option available? Absolutely.

Why don't they? One reason could be lack of understanding, or maybe they are afraid of the confusion that it may cause. The smart employers, however, make this available for young savers, even if it might cost a little more to administer or cause confusion.

Should young savers demand a Roth option? Absolutely. Not only is a Roth 401(k) good for young savers, it will also benefit the owners.

## Will you qualify for a Roth IRA option?

In order to qualify for a tax-free retirement, you will need to ensure that you meet the IRS standards. For example, in order to contribute funds into a Roth IRA, you will need to have earned income for the year.

According to the IRS, earned income is considered to be money that is paid for work that you performed (or in the case of a small business, profit distributions from the business). This income can include:

- Wages
- Salary
- Tips
- Bonuses

- Commissions
- Self-employment income
- Taxable alimony
- Military deferral pay

Earned income does not include things such as dividends or interest from your investments. It also does not include rent that you receive from investment property or income from pension payments.

In addition to having earned income, you will also need to meet certain income limits for the 2016 tax year in order to qualify for a Roth IRA account. These income limits include:

| Chart #9: 2016 Roth IRA Income and Contribution Limits | |
|---|---|
| Roth IRA Contribution Limit - Age 49 and younger | $5,500 |
| Roth IRA Contribution Limit - Age 50 and over | $6,500 |
| Traditional IRA Contribution Limit - Age 49 and younger | $5,500 |
| Traditional IRA Contribution Limit - Age 50 and over | $6,500 |
| Roth IRA Income Limits for Single Filers | Phase-out starts at $117,000 Ineligible at $132,000 |
| Roth IRA Income Limits for Married Filers | Phase-out starts at $184,000 Ineligible at $194,000 |
| Source: RothIRA.com | |

Even if you don't qualify for a Roth IRA based on the income limitations, there is the back-door option as a Roth alternative for you (discussed below and defined in chapter 6), so it will be important to discuss your options with a retirement advisor.

It is also important to note that if you already have a traditional IRA in place, you may be able to convert it over to a Roth. If you convert a traditional IRA to a Roth IRA, you will be required to pay income tax on the conversion amount. Therefore, the taxable amount that is converted over will be added to your regular income tax rate.

However, once you have paid this tax, you will be on your way to earning tax-free returns in your Roth account as well as to having tax-free withdrawals on your future retirement income that you take from the account.

In fact, getting into a Roth IRA sooner rather than later means that you can virtually give yourself the gift of owing no income tax on those funds during your retirement years. So the balance of your portfolio will be the actual amount that can be tapped into in retirement without the need to calculate your "after-tax" balance.

Here is an example of a back-door IRA for everyone to include $500,000 of income or more:

Step 1: Invest a nondeductible $5,500 into a traditional IRA.
Step 2: Soon afterward, convert that into a Roth IRA (no gain, no tax).

Some examples of investment options that can allow you to get years of tax-free compounding include:

- Growth stocks
- Dividend-paying stocks
- Growth mutual funds
- Fixed annuities
- Government bonds

- High-yield corporate bonds
- Real estate
- Variable annuities with income options
- Private equity
- Alternative investments
- Hedge funds

## Scenario 1: Taking a look at a tax-free family

In order to help you understand how the tax-free retirement options work, we are going to look at a fictional couple who have decided to utilize the Roth tax-free plans that are available to them.

Terry and Bob are young, twenty-something professionals. Because they both work full time, they presently have no plans to have children. To start planning for their future retirement savings, they each open Roth IRA accounts (sadly, their employers do not offer Roth 401(k) plans, even though they should and employees are pushing them for this option) so that they can start to save tax-free.

Let's imagine that Terry and Bob are both twenty-five years old and they both put $5,000 annually into their Roth IRAs. We will also assume that the money inside of these Roth IRAs gets an 8 percent return annually.

Even though setting aside $10,000 per year is a stretch for them, Terry and Bob are diligent savers, having their Roth IRA contributions directly deposited straight from their paychecks each month. This "pay yourself first" mentality helps the couple ensure that their money is deposited, allowing their accounts to keep up the momentum.

### Chart 10: $10,000 Per Year

| Terry & Bob's Initial Deposits | $10,000 | At the end of the year... | |
|---|---|---|---|
| End of Year 1 | $10,800 | They make another cumulative $10,000 deposit | |
| End of Year 2 | $22,464 | They make another cumulative $10,000 deposit | |
| End of Year 3 | $35,061 | They make another cumulative $10,000 deposit | |
| End of Year 4 | $48,666 | They make another cumulative $10,000 | |
| End of Year 5 | $63,356 | Total deposits: $50,000 | *At the end of Year 5, Bob and Terry have earned $13,356 of tax-free interest - which is 27% of their deposits!* |

After five years of diligently making their Roth IRA deposits, the account balances are beginning to really pick up steam. This is a great start for Terry and Bob, as the snowball is starting to grow to more than $63,300.

As Terry and Bob continue funding their Roth IRAs, by the end of year ten, the value of their two Roth accounts combined will be $156,000 (assuming the 8 percent annual return). By the end of year twenty, the value of their two Roth IRA accounts will be $494,229—nearly half a million dollars.

So here, by the age of forty-five, the couple will have contributed $200,000 in total, and their tax-free snowball has earned even more than that in interest, with even more tax-free compounding to go.

If they wanted to, they could actually retire at this point. However, because they have no children and are both focused on their careers, Terry and Bob have opted to continue working, funding their accounts, and watching the snowball increase even further.

If the couple decide to retire when they are both sixty-five years old, and their accounts continue earning an 8 percent return over time, they could receive $223,824 in tax-free retirement income each year and have no triggers for tax on their Social Security benefits or the requirement for a higher Medicare Part B premium. (The Social Security tax triggers will be explained in more detail in the next chapter.)

At this point in time, they will have a giant tax-free snowball that has grown to $2,797,810. While Terry and Bob have only made total contributions of $400,000, their tax-free snowball is nearly $3 million. And that is without even having a Roth 401(k) plan through their employers.

Because Terry and Bob made wise choices to start saving early and to maximize their Roth contributions, they could've retired much earlier. Having made smart choices, they not only provided themselves with a nice balance in their portfolio but also with more choices and more control over their futures.

What if Terry and Bob had instead invested in a tax-deferred account? The math calculation with a traditional tax-deferred account for Terry and Bob would allow them to deposit $12,000 as versus $10,000 per year in the tax-free account.

At age 65, the tax-deferred account, growing at 8%, would have grown to $3,357,372 as versus the tax-free account with a future value of $2,797,810. However, if Bob and Terry are in the 30% tax bracket, their lump sum of $3,357,372 from a tax-deferred account would be reduced to $2,350,160 after taxes. But, they would still have the entire $2,797,860 in the tax-free account. This is a net difference of $447,649 in favor of the tax-free account.

*Footnote: The assumptions used in these calculations was a 20% bracket for the deductions in a traditional deferred account. With a yield of $3,357,372 this account is essentially a ticking tax time bomb.

There could, however, be some instances where a tax-deferred account may be favorable. These include:

- If you believe that you will be in a 0% bracket in retirement.
- You plan to leave your tax-deferred account to a charity.
- You do not think you will grow money at 8%.

CHAPTER 4

# Understanding Retirement Distribution Triggers

• • •

WHEN SOCIAL SECURITY WAS CREATED in 1935, it was considered to be one of the best systems available to provide income for retirees. In fact today, even with all of its supposed shortcomings, the system still covers more than 90 percent of all US workers.

Overall, the Social Security system was created and designed to help qualifying Americans with concerns regarding how they would pay their bills when they retired, and ever since its inception, it has become one of the largest government programs in the nation, paying out billions of dollars every year to its recipients.

While many people are familiar with the fact that Social Security pays out retirement income benefits, what they are surprised to learn—oftentimes too late—is that these benefits can be, and more often than not are, taxed.

Most retirees today do not understand that in 1993, Congress passed a law by one vote that 85 percent of Social Security is taxable as ordinary income. The one vote needed to break a fifty-fifty tie was from former vice-president Al Gore. Former president Bill Clinton signed it into law.

Making this benefit taxable allowed the government to reduce Social Security benefits for wealthy and/or high-income participants. This practice of reducing benefits through taxes and higher Medicare premiums is generally referred to as "means testing." The government uses "means testing" to make sure that those who have "enough" income share the costs of keeping the Social Security and Medicare programs solvent.

This differs quite a bit from how the Social Security system was initially intended. In fact, when the very first benefits were paid out back in 1935 to retirees, this income was 100 percent tax-free.

Today, however, it comes as a big surprise to many seniors who use traditional tax-deferred accounts that their retirement distributions from their savings are taxable as ordinary income. As a result, their retirement money *and* Social Security benefits combined fall across the seven tax brackets.

In fact, applying the ordinary income tax rate to these benefits *as if they were ordinary income* essentially ends up netting wealthier individuals *less* in actual benefits. The social benefit is that these government programs remain in force for those who don't have the financial means to retire without the government's help.

In 2016, for instance, a high-income earner might get Social Security retirement benefits of $45,000 per year. This is based on a married couple who qualifies for full benefits. If that high-income earner had a traditional IRA or other taxable account that was paying out large distributions, it could have an effect on how much they pay in taxes on their Social Security benefits.

Let's take a look at what three of the seven tax brackets do to this $45,000 Social Security benefit based on the fact that the retiree also has high taxable income from other sources that puts him into any of these tax brackets:

**Chart #11: Taxable Social Security Benefits on $45,000 in Earnings**

| Tax Bracket | Federal Taxes | Net Social Security Benefit |
|---|---|---|
| 25% | $9,562 | $35,438 |
| 33% | $12,622 | $32,373 |
| 39.6% | $15,147 | $29,853 |

For example, a high-income earner in the 25 percent tax bracket would have to pay income tax not only on his taxable retirement distributions but also on his $45,000 in Social Security benefits, reducing the amount received to only $35,438. Likewise, a high-income earner who is in the 39.6 percent tax bracket would end up paying taxes of more than $15,000 on his Social Security and netting only $29,853 in benefits.

But by doing some advance planning, the Roth tax-free retiree would be able to pay 0 percent income tax on his Roth retirement distributions, as well as no income tax on his Social Security benefits. Zero.

Because money that comes out of a Roth account is tax-free, the person taking money out of it does not fall into any of the seven tax brackets. This is because the withdrawals coming out of a Roth account are not counted as taxable income. Thus, the taxes on the money that come out of this account are $0. It's easy to see how having money in a Roth account can allow you to enjoy your retirement more.

This brings us to yet another important area of concern for retirees: health insurance cost. The government uses means testing here too, making health care more expensive for wealthier retirees in order to pay for the programs.

What is Medicare? Basically, it is the federal health insurance for people age 65 and older. This federal program was started in

1966. Like many federal programs, it started small and became very large.

The first tax rate in the 1930s for Social Security was only 1 percent, and the Medicare tax rate was .35 percent of income—a low total tax of 1.35 percent at the start. Today, the tax is a total of 15.3 percent.

That's because the government can still receive tax revenue to pay for programs like Social Security and Medicare. With that in mind, Uncle Sam decided to do the same thing with Medicare premiums for high-income earners as well.

The government's idea was to create five different levels of income, where the individual in the highest tax bracket would have to pay more for his Medicare Part B and Part D premium than the individual in the lower bracket.

This also fits the concept of means testing, which is now very well established with the Social Security benefit, and it easily became law in order to make Medicare more financially sound. Here are the five levels (for 2016) for married couples (level 1 is for the poorest individual):

Updated Chart 12

**Chart 12: Annual Medicare Costs for Retirees on Part B and Part D**

| Level Based on Income | 65-Year-Old Couples |
|---|---|
| 1 (for the poorest) | $2,923 |
| 2 | $4,396 |
| 3 | $6,633 |
| 4 | $8,868 |
| 5 (for the wealthiest) | $11,104 |

This is very much a part of the current tax system today, and it now is easily adjusted with tax brackets and cost levels based on an individual's taxable income.

So what is the key point here, especially in terms of avoiding a big potential tax hit on your Social Security retirement income in the future?

First and foremost, tax-free Roth accounts are best for young savers. If you have the option to choose between Roth and tax-deferred savings, Roth is certainly the better way to go, even though you aren't able to deduct your contributions into the account.

The government now has in place a very effective means testing on ordinary income, and it would be easy to change all brackets by 3.8 percent. So, for instance, instead of 10 percent, a tax of 13.8 percent might seem "fair." And 39.6 percent could be adjusted upward to a tax of 44.4 percent in the future. It's a simple revenue approach.

*The most successful income earners could essentially see their $45,000 Social Security benefit magically turn into a low net of only $18,772.* This is after income tax and the cost of medical insurance, *ultimately a 58 percent total reduction in government benefits.* This is another big reason why tax-free is the main objective.

If a tax-deferred savings account is the only option that you have, for instance, through your employer-sponsored plan, then certainly go that route. Just keep in mind that you will want to convert these funds over to a Roth down the road so that you can take advantage of the tax-free withdrawals at retirement.

CHAPTER 5

# Life Insurance—The Ultimate Tax-Free Planning Vehicle

• • •

TO MANY YOUNG SAVERS, THE purchase of life insurance might seem like something that you can take care of "later on." After all, you're young and you have your whole life ahead of you, right? Why worry about such depressing topics now?

The reality is that life insurance can be both important and beneficial regardless of how young and healthy you are right now. Unfortunately, the unexpected can and sometimes does happen. And if it does, you don't want to leave those you care about without the financial means to go on.

Many healthy thirty-year-olds don't realize that by simply paying about $40 per month, they can ensure that their family is protected financially with $500,000. This could keep loved ones from having to dip into savings or other assets in order to cover the cost of final expenses, pay off large debts, and address many other pressing financial hardships that could potentially devastate their lifestyle going forward.

Think about it this way. If you were to take $40 per month and put it into a mutual fund—even a fund that was generating a nice return of say 10 or 12 percent per year—how long would it take you to build up your account to $500,000 or $1 million? Actually, at 10 percent, it would take you more than forty-eight years to get to $500,000![1]

When you have life insurance, though, from the minute your policy is approved by the insurance company, should something happen to you, your beneficiary will be financially protected with the policy's death benefit proceeds.

But let's just say that you *were* able to "hit it big" with a tax-deferred stock or a mutual fund, and your $40 per month investment somehow climbed to $500,000. And then the unthinkable happened. Unfortunately, depending on who inherited your money, a large portion of it would still be going to Uncle Sam in the form of taxes. That's because the return on most investment accounts is taxable.

In fact, depending on the tax bracket, as much as $140,000 or even $175,000 may have to be handed over in taxes and therefore diverted away from your family. If you had saved up $1 million, then, depending on the tax bracket, there could be up to $396,000 taken out in the form of taxes.

That doesn't seem like a very good deal for your family—especially if they could have used that money to pay off debt or for their ongoing living expenses. But this wouldn't happen if the money was inherited as a life insurance benefit. In that case, the entire $500,000 or $1 million could be received tax-free to be used for whatever your loved ones want or need.

## How Life Insurance Works

Life insurance coverage has actually changed a great deal over the years. While the basic concept has remained the same, the ability to customize policies in order to meet various needs has significantly expanded.

There are two primary categories of life insurance coverage. These are term and permanent. With term life insurance, you get pure life insurance protection without any of the other "bells and whistles," like savings or investments that are attached to the policy—and because of this, term life insurance can typically be an extremely affordable way to obtain a nice amount of coverage. This is especially the case if you are young and in good health when you apply for the policy.

Term life insurance, as the name implies, is purchased for a certain length of time—or "term"—such as ten, twenty, or even thirty years. In most cases, the premium will remain level during the term of coverage. And in some cases, depending on the policy that you purchase, you may have the option to convert the term insurance coverage over into a permanent life insurance policy. You may even be able to do this without having to take a medical exam or even to prove evidence of insurability.

The benefit of doing this in the future is that it could provide you with a life insurance policy for the remainder of your lifetime (provided that the premium continues to be paid), in case you were to contract an adverse health condition and become uninsurable down the road. In other cases, the term policy will simply expire.

Permanent life insurance provides death benefit protection along with a cash value component. These policies offer coverage that is intended to remain in force for the rest of your life, as long as premiums are paid.

The cash within the policy is allowed to grow tax deferred. This means, similar to with a traditional IRA or 401(k) account, that the funds inside of the life insurance policy aren't taxed unless or until they are withdrawn.

Because of this cash component, though, the premiums that are charged for a permanent life insurance policy can be significantly more than those of a comparable term insurance policy, all other factors being equal. (We will discuss permanent insurance, and how it can be used in various financial planning situations, in more detail later in this book.)

## Do You Really Need Life Insurance?

While most people don't like to talk about it, a discussion about life insurance is one of those necessary evils that need to be included in order to ensure that your overall financial plan is complete. This is especially the case if you have anyone in your life who depends on you for financial support.

First and foremost, it is important to note that life insurance coverage isn't necessarily just for the person who is insured; it is for the people who are left behind. These are the ones who will need to deal with the unpaid debt and/or the ongoing living expenses—financial hardships that could be made much easier with income tax–free funds from a life insurance policy.

In fact, just a quick look on GoFundMe.com will take you to a stark reality of the multitude of families who are in need of money for the funeral or other financial obligations of a young loved one who died unexpectedly. These people also never thought it would ever happen to them. But it did.

Even if you have life insurance as part of a group benefits plan through your employer, this coverage is oftentimes not nearly enough. You will also typically lose that coverage if you leave your employer.

Many people may also qualify to get survivor benefits from Social Security if a loved one passes away. Although these benefits are tax-free, the amount of those benefits may not be nearly enough to support your family in the way that you intend.

So do you need life insurance? Well, you might actually need it for a number of reasons, including:

- Final expenses—Regardless of how young or old someone is, funerals and other related expenses can be quite costly. Today, the nationwide average funeral cost is right around $10,000 when factoring in a burial plot, headstone, casket, memorial service, flowers, and transportation.
- Unpaid debt—You may also have unpaid debt such as a mortgage that you would like to have paid off if something should happen to you. That way, if you have a spouse and young children, they may continue to live in the home without having to uproot. This can be particularly helpful, especially during an already difficult time for them.
- Ongoing Living Expenses—Whether you're the primary income earner in your household or you share expenses with a spouse or partner, the loss of your income could be disruptive or even devastating to the living situation of others. If that is the case, the proceeds from a life insurance policy can help those you leave behind to go on, continuing to meet expenses going forward.

It's important to note here that if you are part of a couple where one spouse or partner is the primary income earner and the other is a stay-at-home spouse or partner whose job is to take care of the home and the kids, the loss of the non–income earner can also be devastating financially. This is because it can be extremely costly to replace an individual who provided cooking, cleaning, and childcare.

There are numerous reasons for life insurance. Yet because all situations can differ, the amount of coverage that you need should be carefully determined in order to ensure that your loved ones have enough. Meeting with a qualified financial advisor can help you to more closely determine just how much coverage you may require.

## THE TAX-FREE ADVANTAGES OF LIFE INSURANCE

In addition to the fact that life insurance can allow your loved ones to go on financially, it can also do so without your beneficiary (or beneficiaries) having to split those proceeds with Uncle Sam. That is because when life insurance proceeds are received by your beneficiary, there are no income taxes at either the federal or the state level. This means that your beneficiaries will be able to use the full 100 percent of the benefit that they receive from the policy. In other words, when life insurance benefits are paid out in a lump sum, this amount does not need to be included in the gross income of the beneficiary.

This alone can be huge. Imagine, for instance, if the unthinkable occurred. If you owned a life insurance policy with a $1 million benefit, would you rather that your family inherited the entire $1 million or that they "shared" $280,000 or $350,000 (or more) of that money with the government?

## WHICH TYPE OF LIFE INSURANCE IS RIGHT FOR YOU?

While there are many different types of life insurance that are available in the market today, the reality is that finding the right coverage for you doesn't need to be difficult. That is because in many cases, especially when you are just starting out, you can often obtain what you need with a good, solid term insurance plan.

For example, a twenty-year term life insurance policy with a benefit of $500,000 or even $1 million can help to ensure that your loved ones won't have to endure financial hardship going forward or drastically change their lives if the unexpected occurs. And if you're thinking that a benefit of $500,000—or even coverage of $1 million—is way too much, then you may want to think again. Here's why.

Let's say you're purchasing life insurance for the purpose of protecting your young family. You have a stay-at-home spouse and two children, both under five years old. In today's low-interest-rate environment, $1 million invested at 2 percent or even at 3 percent will get you somewhere between $20,000 and $30,000 per year in interest.

Would your family be able to live on that amount of interest per year?

Ideally, you would be able to live off the interest. You could, however, use the principal as well for certain needs such as paying off debt, funding future education expenses, or various other financial obligations.

## How much will this protection cost?

There are a number of different factors that go into pricing a life insurance policy. Some of the primary criteria include the type of coverage that you're purchasing (e.g., term or permanent), as well as the amount of the policy's benefit.

Your age, gender, and health can also play a part in the price of your coverage. For instance, the cost of life insurance is based in large part on life expectancy. Because life insurance companies don't want to take big risks on unhealthy people as this could result in having to pay out costly claims, they will generally price their policies lower for young, healthier people and higher for those who are older and who have various health issues.

Also, if you are a male, you will likely pay more for your coverage than if you are a female. That is because, on average, females live longer than males. (Sorry, guys.) When it comes to other types of insurance coverage, however, such as long-term care, women will pay more in premiums due to their longer life expectancy.

So just how much will it all cost?

Let's take an example of a thirty-year-old nonsmoking male who is looking for a $500,000 term life insurance policy with a twenty-year benefit period. Being in just average health, this individual could obtain coverage for approximately $40 per month. But if he is in excellent health, he can obtain this half-million dollars in life insurance coverage for less than $25 per month.

What if this same individual who is in great health raises the coverage amount to $1 million? Well, he can then lock in twenty years of term life coverage with several top-rated carriers for less than $40 per month.[2]

Most people spend more than that regularly on cocktails, going to a movie, or other trivial items, often without even thinking about it. So why wouldn't you provide those you love with financial protection that could mean the difference between keeping their lives the same or drastically altering their futures?

## Scenario 2: Working life insurance into your plan

In seeing how you can work life insurance into your overall financial plan, let's take a look at another fictional couple, Alice and Joe. They got married approximately ten years ago, when they were in their midtwenties. Now they are in their midthirties and are starting a family.

Alice and Joe, both age thirty, have been smart savers, and both have set up Roth IRAs, allowing their tax-free savings to build up—and they plan to continue funding these accounts in the future. Like Terry and Bob, this couple are able to grow their Roth IRA balances to a combined $156,000+, so their snowball is also starting to grow.

They each also have life insurance through their employers. But with their plans for a family moving forward, they know that they will need additional coverage. This is because the amount of coverage through their employer is not nearly enough. In addition, if either of them were to lose their job, they would also lose that life insurance protection.

The couple, with both working out on a regular basis and in very good health, know that they should have no problem qualifying for the life insurance that they need. However, Alice and Joe also realize that just in case Alice encounters any health issues with her pregnancy, it is best for her to apply for coverage sooner better than later. This is because one of the biggest criteria in being approved for life insurance is your health condition.

Therefore, Alice and Joe contact their financial advisor, and they each apply for a twenty-year term life insurance policy with a death benefit of $500,000. Now, for less than $40 per month apiece—the cost of just one dinner at a restaurant—if something were to happen to either of them, the other would be able to pay off the balance of their home mortgage, as well as have additional funds for future college education costs and other needs.

Chart #13: Value of Insurance and Investments Over Time

| Age | Tax-Free Death Benefit on Term Life Insurance Policy | 2 Roth IRA values* |
|---|---|---|
| 35 | $500,000 | $156,000 |
| 45 | $500,000 | $500,000 |
| 55 | $500,000 | $1,200,000 |
| 65 | $0 | $3,000,000 |

Here, just as with Terry and Bob, it is easy to see how Alice and Joe's snowball grows exponentially over the years. And when they are ready to retire, they will have the ability to receive ongoing retirement income from their Roth IRA accounts without having to pay taxes to Uncle Sam.

1. Roth assets will pass tax-free to beneficiaries. A traditional IRA and/or pension will pass to beneficiaries at 100 percent taxable income.
2. Male, five foot ten, 165 pounds, nonsmoker, twenty-year guaranteed level term, monthly premium mode. Source: truebluelifeinsurance.com.

CHAPTER 6

# Saving for College Using Tax-Free Strategies

• • •

IN ADDITION TO SAVING FOR retirement, there are other methods of both accumulating and withdrawing tax-free funds. One way that you can potentially build up a substantial sum—provided that you start early and make regular contributions—is by having a 529 plan.

A 529 plan is defined as an education savings plan that is operated by either a state or an educational institution. These plans are essentially designed to help families set aside money for future college expenses. Just like many other types of savings plans, 529 plans got their name from the Internal Revenue Code section that created them.

Opening a 529 plan can be essential if you have anyone in your life who will be encountering the cost of college in the future. This is because other than retirement and a home mortgage, the cost of higher education may be the biggest expense that most people will face in their lifetime.

Based on a study by Campus Consultants, Inc., as the cost of college continues to skyrocket, you could be looking at a six-figure-per-year price tag in the future, depending on where your child decides to attend.

Chart #14: Projected Tuition Costs Fall 2029-Spring 2030

| School Type | 5% increases | 6% increases | 7% increases |
|---|---|---|---|
| 4-Year Public (out of state) | $71,373 | $84,651 | $100,239 |
| 4-Year Private (non-profit) | $92,869 | $110,146 | $130,428 |
| 4-Year Public (in-state) | $41,228 | $48,898 | $57,609 |

Source: Campus Consultants, Inc.

*Includes the cost of room and board.

## How exactly do 529 plans work?

A 529 plan can allow for a way to save money for future college costs. These plans permit you to either prepay the tuition at a qualified educational institution at current tuition rates or to invest funds into a tax-free account that will let the money be used for qualifying education expenses at future tuition rates.

(Per the IRS, a qualified educational institution is generally considered to be any college, university, vocational school, or other postsecondary educational institution that is eligible to participate in a student-aid program that is administered by the United States Department of Education.)

With a state-sponsored 529 savings plan, the state actually sets up the plan with an asset-management company of its choosing. You can then establish a plan with such a company. In this case, the asset-management company would set up the plan according to the predetermined requisites of your state.

However, because there are no residency requirements with regard to 529 plans, you can invest in any state's plan regardless of where you live. In addition, the assets that are in a 529 plan can be used to pay for higher education in any state. In other words, even if you live in Missouri, your choice of educational institution won't be affected by the state that your 529 plan is from. You can be a Missouri resident, invest in a California plan, and send your child to a college in Massachusetts if you so desire.

A 529 college plan may be opened through any of the states' higher educational savings websites; however, it is typically better if you work with a qualified financial advisor who can walk you through your best course of action on these plans, since there can be many moving parts.

## Types of 529 Plans

There are actually two different types of 529 plans: prepaid tuition plans and savings plans. Also, each individual state may have its own plan, although states are allowed to offer both types of plans. However, plans that are offered via qualified educational institutions can only be the prepaid-tuition type.

It is important to be aware of the differences between the two types of 529 plans because there are several differences, including:

- **Prepaid tuition plans:** A prepaid tuition plan allows prepayment of either all or part of the cost of an in-state public college. These types of plans may also be converted over for use at either a private and/or an out-of-state educational institution. There is also a type of private-college 529 plan available. This is a plan in which a separate, prepaid higher-educational savings plan is specifically geared toward saving for the cost of a private college or university.

- **Savings plans:** A savings plan works in a somewhat similar manner to an IRA or a 401(k) retirement plan in that the funds that are within the account may be invested in a variety of different financial vehicles. In these types of plans, the account value may rise and fall based upon the performance of the underlying investments that have been chosen.

In either the prepaid tuition plan or the savings plan, the account holder may earn interest on the underlying investments that are inside of the account.

Chart #15: A Comparison of Prepaid Tuition Plans and 529 Savings Plans

| Prepaid Tuition Plan | 529 Savings Plan |
| --- | --- |
| Locks in tuition prices at eligible public and private colleges and universities. | No lock on college costs. |
| All plans cover tuition and mandatory fees only. Some plans allow a room and board option, or may allow use of excess tuition credits for other qualified expenses. | Covers all "qualified higher education expenses," including:<br>• Tuition<br>• Room & Board<br>• Mandatory Fees<br>• Books<br>• Computers and related equipment |
| Most plans set lump sum and installment payments prior to purchase based on the age of the beneficiary and the number of years of college tuition purchased. | Many plans have contribution limits in excess of $200,000. |
| Many plans are backed or guaranteed by the state. | No state guarantee. Most investment options are subject to market risk. Investment may make no profit - or may even decline in value. |
| Most plans have age and/or grade limits for the beneficiary. | No age limits. Open to adults and children. |
| Most plans require either the account holder or the beneficiary to be a state resident. | No residency requirement. However, nonresidents may only be able to purchase some plans through financial advisors or brokers. |
| Most plans have a limited enrollment period. | Enrollment is open all year. |

Source: "Smart Saving for College," NASD.

The important difference here is that with the 529 savings plan, you have much, much more flexibility in terms of where you use the money (for example, no residency requirements), and you can even pass the money on to future generations. You aren't able to do that with a prepaid plan. In most cases, the 529 savings plan is really the best way to go.

## THE TAX-FREE ADVANTAGES OF COLLEGE 529 PLANS

There are a number of benefits to investing through a college 529 plan. Certainly it can help you to establish a way for a loved one to have the funding that he or she needs to attend the school of his or her choice. However, another key advantage of these plans is the fact that the earnings within them are not subject to federal income taxation. In addition, these earnings may also be exempt from state income tax when they are used for paying certain types of qualified educational expenses for the account beneficiary.

These qualifying expenses can include the following:

- Tuition
- Fees
- Books
- Room and board
- Certain computer equipment

Furthermore, even though the contributions that go into a college 529 plan are not tax deductible, the funds that are inside of the account are allowed to grow without being taxed. And the distributions that are made to the account beneficiary—and that are used for qualifying expenses—can come out federally tax-free and sometimes even free of state income tax too.

Because of this, even if the money is used for other purposes, you will not be required to report the earnings on the assets from this account until the year in which they are withdrawn. In addition, there are some states that may also offer certain other tax breaks. So it is important to check with your tax advisor.

## OTHER BENEFITS OF INVESTING IN A 529 PLAN

In addition to the tax-free aspect, there are other nice benefits that can go along with investing in 529 plans. For example, these plans are, for the most part, extremely easy to set up and contribute to.

Also, because the ongoing administration of these plans is handled by the plan itself, and the assets are professionally managed by either an investment company or the office of the state treasurer, a 529 plan can be very low maintenance.

These plans are also flexible. Investment options that are in the plan may be changed twice per calendar year, and you are allowed to roll over your funds into another 529 plan one time in a twelve-month period.

Additionally, unlike some of the tax-free (and tax-deferred) retirement plan options that we have discussed so far in the book, everyone is eligible to take advantage of a 529 college-savings plan. This isn't so with all the retirement plans, based on your age and/or your annual income amount.

You are also able to contribute a fairly substantial amount into a 529 plan. For example, there are lifetime contribution limits that vary—and the amounts can differ by plan—but you may be able to deposit somewhere in the range of $200,000 to $500,000.

## When should you set up a 529 college-savings plan?

Just as with any other type of savings plan, the best time to set up a 529 college-savings plan is sooner rather than later. This is especially the case if you have already started a family. An earlier head start allows more time for the funds in the account to snowball.

**Chart #16: Saving Monthly Goes a Long Way**

Over time, a little goes a long way.

| | 5 years | 10 years | 15 years | 18 years |
|---|---|---|---|---|
| $15 a month | $1,080 | $2,600 | $4,800 | $6,500 |
| $50 a month | $3,600 | $8,700 | $15,900 | $21,700 |
| $100 a month | $7,200 | $17,400 | $31,900 | $43,300 |

This chart is a hypothetical example and should not be considered an indication of performance of a 529 plan. These estimates assume that contributions of $15, $50, and $100 per month are made at the beginning of the month with a 7% annual return. Assumes that the money is invested in a tax-free investment vehicle, such as a 529 plan.

Source: Why Save for College? - Cost of College & Saving for College - CSPN

## What if you have money left over?

According to the College Board, costs for a public college education for the 2013–2014 school year averaged nearly $23,000. However, if your child is still just a baby, you may be faced with a total college cost of more than $230,000 in eighteen years.

Using the funds that you build up in a 529 plan to help pay the cost of college tuition and fees, room and board, books and supplies, and even computers (and related equipment) can really help, especially given the plan's tax-advantaged status.

So what if you still have excess funds in your 529 plan even after paying all these costs? There are some things that you can do in order to continue taking advantage of your 529 plan benefits.

One would be to change the plan's beneficiary to another qualifying family member who may be planning to attend college in the future. That way, the money in the 529 plan's account could then be used for paying his or her expenses. That other beneficiary could also include yourself, in the case that you may wish to further your own education down the road.

You could also leave the plan as is in case the current beneficiary decides to attend graduate school at some time in the future. Today, many college students opt to continue their education beyond a bachelor's degree.

While it is difficult to know exactly what will happen in the future, having a long-term plan in place can help you to be prepared financially for many of the what-ifs in life. Working with a qualified financial professional who can design a plan for you based on your specific goals will get you moving in the right direction.

## Scenario 2: Extended for adding a 529 college-savings plan

When our fictional couple Alice and Joe started a family, in addition to purchasing life insurance for protection, the couple also began putting $50 per month into a 529 college-savings plan for each of their two children as soon as each one was born.

Alice and Joe knew that all the money that they deposit into these plans is allowed to grow on a tax-free basis. And if it is invested well, assuming an average 7 percent return, after eighteen years, each plan will have more than $20,000 in it that can be put toward the cost of education and/or related expenses.

| Chart #17: Alice and Joe's Plan | | | |
|---|---|---|---|
| Age | Tax-Free Death Benefit on Term Life Insurance Policy | 2 Roth IRA Accounts | Tax-Free Balance on 529 College Saving Plan |
| 35 | $500,000 | $156,000 | $2,400 |
| 45 | $500,000 | $500,000 | $34,800 |
| 55 | $500,000 | $1,200,000 | $86,000 |

Because Alice and Joe opted for the 529 savings plan versus the prepaid tuition plan, it actually gave them more options, which is a good thing. This is because their younger son, Jeff, opted to go to technical school rather than to attend Duke, which is where his parents had initially intended that he go. So, in addition to the tax-free benefits that can be obtained with a 529 savings plan, it also provides you with more flexibility.

CHAPTER 7

# Affluent Millennials

• • •

THIS BOOK IS AIMED AT all young savers, who equal roughly 150 million of our youngest working generation. So far, we have covered the tax-free steps that every millennial should try to take as he or she grows.

In this chapter, we will cover what the highest-income earners should ideally add to their tax-free foundation while they are still in their peak earning years. Their foundation should include the following:

* **Step 1:** Roth IRAs and Roth 401(k)s. Some experts may say that your income is too high to have a Roth IRA. However, if you fall into this category, there is such a thing as a "back-door" Roth for affluent income earners (introduced in chapter 3). A back-door IRA allows you to get around income limits by converting a traditional IRA into a Roth IRA. People who earn too much income are not allowed to open Roth IRAs; however, in order to still obtain a Roth IRA—and all the tax-free income benefits that go along with it—you can initially make a contribution to a traditional IRA and then convert it over. Also, if your employer does not already offer a Roth 401(k) option, check with your HR

department and other higher-ups to see what needs to be done in order to obtain one in your employee benefits.
- **Step 2:** Term life insurance. Having term life insurance coverage is a must for affluent young savers with families. There is absolutely nothing wrong with obtaining up to $5 million in tax-free protection if you can afford the premium and you can qualify health-wise for the coverage.
- **Step 3:** College savings. A 529 college-savings plan is also a must, especially for high-tax-bracket couples, in order to grow money tax-free for future college education expenses. This type of plan can also provide you with a great deal of flexibility in terms of the education-related costs that it can be used for.

*Note: When this book makes statements regarding qualified advisors and companies, we base this on our knowledge and experience. Any advisor with a DNA that is similar to A. G. Edwards's legacy of "client first" is highly recommended by us. We also use and recommend companies like USAA and TIAA-CREF, along with their advisors.*

## Following the rules of tax-free investing is very important

When we say tax-free, we must reiterate that there are certain rules that must be followed in order to ensure that you are able to obtain the full benefits of these plans. While they are not hard rules to follow, they must nevertheless be adhered to. For example, a 529 college plan has to be used for college-related expenses, not for buying a boat.

Likewise, when you purchase life insurance, the beneficiary must have what is referred to as an insurable interest in the insured. This means that the beneficiary must suffer some sort of financial loss or hardship if the insured were to die. So it is important that the named beneficiary have an insurable interest in the insured. In the purchase of life insurance coverage, family protection should typically be the number-one reason for obtaining a policy.

Although we discussed the fact that term life insurance was a great way for young families and individuals to obtain a large amount of death benefit, usually for a very affordable premium, for those who are higher-income earners, permanent life insurance can be a great way to build up tax-deferred cash value.

Permanent life insurance provides both death-benefit protection and a cash value component. These policies offer coverage that is intended to remain in force for the rest of the insured's life, as long as premiums are paid.

The cash within the policy is allowed to grow tax deferred. This means, similar to a traditional IRA or 401(k) account, that the funds inside of the life insurance policy aren't taxed unless or until they are withdrawn.

Because of this cash component, though, the premiums that are charged for a permanent life insurance policy can be significantly more than those of a comparable term life insurance policy, all other factors being equal.

There are many different types of permanent and dividend-paying permanent life insurance coverage, including:

* **Whole life insurance**: Whole life, also often referred to as ordinary life or straight life insurance, is the most basic of permanent life insurance policies. With this coverage, the

premium will typically remain the same throughout the entire length of the policy. The cash value component grows based on a minimum guaranteed rate of return that is set by the offering insurance company. In some cases, a whole life insurance policy may also offer dividends that can be used to increase the cash value or to purchase additional amounts of insurance coverage.

These dividends represent a portion of the insurance company's profits that are paid out to policyholders. There are several different options when it comes to using your life insurance dividends. For example, you could simply request that the insurance company send you a check. Alternatively, you may request that the dividend be put toward paying some or all of your policy's future premium that is due. Yet another option is to keep the dividend in the policy's cash value so that it can help to increase its total value.

The dividends that are received from the insurance company are not subject to income tax. This is because they are treated as a refund for overpayment of the premium. Therefore, if premiums are kept inside of the policy's cash value component, they can help to enhance its overall amount over time.

While it is important to note that dividends are not guaranteed, there are some insurance companies that have paid out dividends to their policyholders for many years and some for several decades. These include Northwestern Mutual and New York Life. Throughout the years, though, many mutual insurance companies—those that pay out dividends to their policyholders—have converted over to stock companies and no longer pay out policy dividends. With that in mind, it is important to carefully choose your life insurance policy based on your goals for what you want the policy to do. A qualified advisor can help you to narrow down your best options.

- **Universal life insurance**: Universal life insurance also offers a death benefit and a cash value component. This type of coverage has often been described as providing the low-cost benefit of term life insurance with a cash value like whole life. With these policies, there is a great deal of flexibility.

  For example, you are allowed to change, within certain guidelines, the timing of the premium payments. You may also be able to determine how much of each premium payment goes into the cash value and how much goes toward the death benefit, and you can even move funds between the two sections of the policy.

- **Variable universal life insurance:** Variable universal life insurance is another form of permanent life insurance. Here, you may invest the cash portion of your policy into various investment vehicles, such as mutual funds. If the cash value is invested in vehicles that perform well over time, the amount inside the policy could increase substantially. Unlike a regular investment, if the unexpected should occur, the policy's beneficiary will still receive the benefit proceeds free of income taxation.

This means that they could end up netting significantly more than if they were to inherit funds from that regular account. What exactly do we mean? Let's say that a thirty-year-old has an extra $5,000 per year to purchase a cash value type of life insurance policy. This will purchase him a permanent policy with a permanent death benefit of $500,000. In this case, if his investment grows inside of the life insurance umbrella, it grows tax deferred, or without having to pay any tax on the gain unless or until it is withdrawn. If the insured were to pass away, then the entire $500,000 of death benefit would go to his heir's income, tax-free. Had $500,000 that was inside of a tax-deferred retirement account gone to his heirs, it would have been taxable as ordinary income.

Let's say that an individual owns a variable universal life insurance policy for many years. These policies, which are still really just a combination of term life insurance with an investment element, are interesting. If the insured owns the policy for twenty-five years and pays in $125,000, his investment within the policy may be worth $300,000 at that time. Because of that, the amount of life insurance is really only worth $200,000 ($500,000 minus the savings of $300,000, which can easily be seen on the quarterly or annual insurance statement).

- **Indexed universal life insurance:** With indexed universal life insurance, the performance of the cash value is linked to the performance of an underlying market index, such as the S&P 500. Therefore, when the underlying index performs well, the cash component will rise in value, usually up to a certain upper limit, or "cap." Many indexed universal life insurance policies will also provide some type of assurance of principal protection if the index performs poorly during a given time period.

- **Survivorship policies (second to die)**: Survivorship life insurance policies cover two people's lives. In many instances, these policies will cover two spouses and are used for estate-planning purposes. Here, the policy's benefits are not paid until the survivor, or the second person, passes away.

  With a survivorship policy, the premium is generally lower than if you were to purchase two separate life insurance policies. Also, you may find that the underwriting requirements are less stringent, especially if one of the individuals is in excellent health.

While many people may not consider using life insurance as a wealth-enhancing vehicle, the reality is that the cash inside of a life insurance policy—especially one that allows growth type of investments—has the opportunity to increase significantly over time.

For example, $10,000 invested into the American Funds Investment Company of America mutual fund back in 1934 would have produced phenomenal results of 12% compounded annually. But even over just the past twenty years—which included an economic recession, war, and global economic turmoil—the overall return would have been substantial.

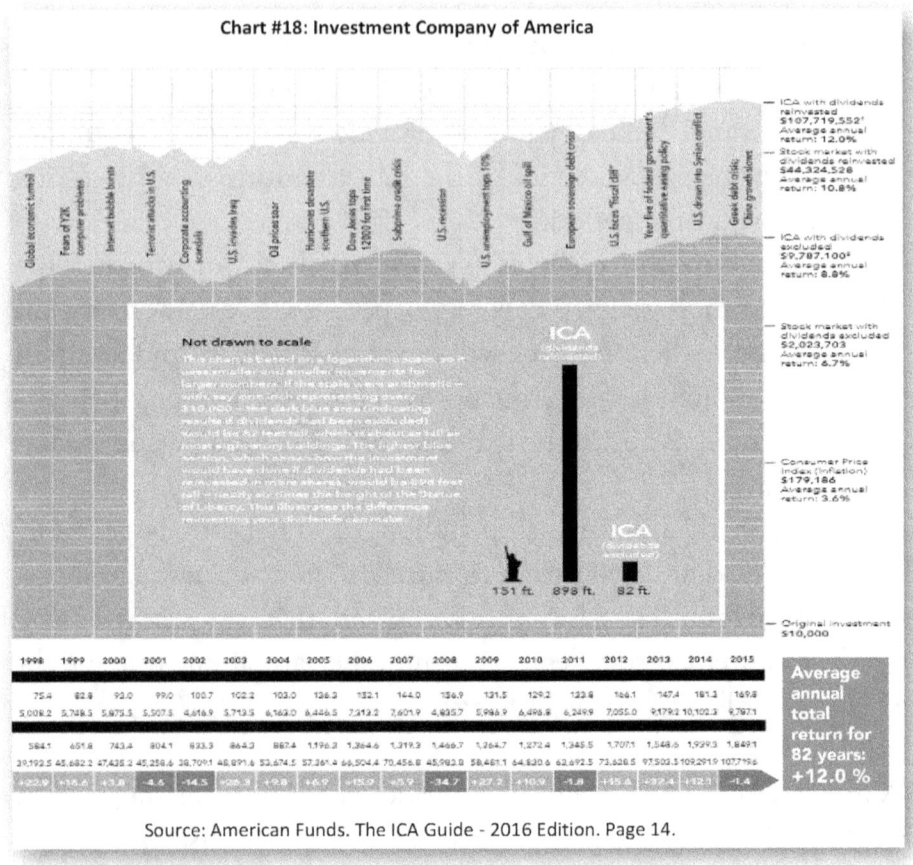

Source: American Funds. The ICA Guide - 2016 Edition. Page 14.

During down times, it may be tempting to get out of the market. But as you can see, the market goes both ways. A good, qualified financial advisor can help you to get through the down periods. Also, by being well diversified, you can also hedge your risk. Here, too, a good advisor can help.

## Donor-advised funds

Another type of tax-free planning tool for affluent taxpayers is a charitable-giving fund. These funds allow donors to make a charitable contribution, receive an immediate tax benefit, and then recommend grants from the fund over time. Many individuals understand that giving to charities is not only good for the charities but also good for their own tax situation, so it can turn out to be a win-win for all.

An easy way to think about donor-advised funds is like a charitable savings account. For example, the donor contributes to the fund as frequently as she would like and then recommends grants to her favorite charity whenever she is ready.

In essence, a donor-advised fund works like this:

- First, you make an irrevocable contribution of assets.
- Next, you immediately receive a tax deduction, which is actually the maximum deduction that is allowed by the IRS.
- You then name your donor-advised fund account, advisors, and any successors or charitable beneficiaries.
- The contribution that you make is placed into a donor-advised fund account, where it may then be invested and grow on a tax-free basis.
- Any time after that, you may recommend grants from the account to qualified charities.

For someone who is in the 39.6 percent tax bracket, it would technically only "cost" $6,040 to contribute. Plus, the entire $10,000 goes into a fund that grows tax-free. After ten years of, say, an 8 percent return, it could be worth in excess of $156,000. After that, the family can give to charities as they wish.

If this same individual had paid taxes and invested in this same tax bracket, he would only have approximately $80,000 saved in a taxable account, so you can see that the future giving fund is almost double.

This approach of using tax deductions and tax-free compounding is what wealthy families like the Buffetts and the Clintons do. There is absolutely nothing wrong with a family-giving fund for affluent taxpayers.

## Flip a traditional IRA to a Roth

Another way to help yourself avoid a potentially huge tax liability in the future is to convert your traditional IRA account over to a Roth. While you will have a current tax liability for doing so now, it will likely be peanuts compared to the income tax that you would have to pay on your future income in retirement. That is because if you stick with the traditional IRA, you would be taxed on the entire amount that you withdraw from the traditional IRA as versus having tax-free income with the Roth.

In fact, even though the funds inside of a traditional IRA can grow tax deferred, they are essentially just a ticking time bomb as far as the future income tax liability that you would have to pay in retirement. Also, do not forget that these distributions can trigger taxes on your Social Security benefit and increase Medicare costs.

Taking it a step further, if, for instance, an affluent individual has $10,000 in a ticking-time-bomb traditional IRA account, he can switch it over to a Roth. Of course, the $10,000 is considered ordinary income. But he can take a $10,000 cash donation into his new giving fund. This offset would cause no taxes if he is in the 39.6 percent tax bracket. And at the end of the IRA "flip," he would have $10,000 in a tax-free Roth and $10,000 in his tax-free giving account.

## Scenario 3: Putting all the pieces together—an example of successful affluent young savers

After considering all the strategies we have discussed so far, let's take a look at another fictional couple, Ken and Mary. This couple has a fast-growing small business. At age thirty, the couple sets up a Roth 401(k) for themselves, which allowed both of them to invest $17,500 for a total of $35,000 each year.

They were lucky to find the 401(k) retirement plan for businesses that offers a Roth option, as this is an amazing option that many employers do not offer to savers. Even young, low-tax-bracket individuals should be using the Roth 401(k) or the Roth 403(b) options at age twenty-five or so. Tax-free compounding is great for all the tax brackets.

The couple's Roth 401(k) annual contributions can now grow to more than $4.2 million when they reach age sixty, based on a total contribution of just over $1 million and an annual return of 8 percent.

For their two children, Ken and Mary invest $100,000 into a 529 college-savings plan, which ends up growing to more than $400,000 by the time the couple reach age sixty. Since the couple did not use all the money in the college-savings account for their own children, they can now pass on the surplus to their grandchildren for their college expenses tax-free.

Similar to the other fictional couples, Ken and Mary know that they need to protect their loved ones in case of the unexpected. So at age thirty-five, each spouse purchases a thirty-year-term life insurance policy with a $2 million death benefit. This will take them through to age sixty-five.

Also at age sixty, their family-giving fund contributions of $10,000 every year is now over $1 million. This tax-free account can be used for family charity giving not only by Ken and Mary but also by their children.

Ken and Mary learned some of their investment strategies and techniques from financial greats like Warren Buffett, who also follows many of these paths, such as compounding tax-free in order to avoid paying the federal government a lot in taxes. He and his family decide what charities they will support rather than have anyone else do so, including Uncle Sam.

In addition to their other investments, the two permanent life insurance policies that Ken and Mary purchased many years ago now have cash values that have built up, tax deferred, to over $400,000. The couple have a number of options for what they can do with these policies, so they will discuss with their qualified advisor what will be best for them, taking into account possible future needs, such as health care.

The couple's overall results at age sixty include four tax-free accounts that are worth more than *$6 million*, that are continuing to snowball for their family, and that have no triggers for Social Security tax or higher premiums on Medicare.

Chart #19: Ken and Mary's Results at Age 60

| Age | Roth 401(k) Balances (Combined) | 529 College Savings Plan | Tax-Free Buildup Inside the Life Insurance Policy | Giving Fund Balance | |
|---|---|---|---|---|---|
| 60 | $4,200,000 | $400,000 | $400,000 each | $1 million+ | |
| Total Tax-Free Assets | | | | | $6 million |

At this point, the couple could retire if they choose to do so. Here again, by getting an early start and investing in tax-free vehicles, Ken and Mary have not only given themselves a nice portfolio balance, but they also have the benefit of much more control over what they do and when they do it in their lives.

While we know that this example demonstrates just a small percentage of highly paid savers, we also know that if you plan ahead and plan wisely, and if you use these tools as designed, wonderful things can happen.

CHAPTER 8

# Inheriting Tax-Deferred and Tax-Free Assets

• • •

IT HAS BEEN ESTIMATED THAT over the next few decades, more than $30 trillion in assets will pass from baby boomers to their heirs, who are primarily young savers. Yes, that's trillion with a *t*.[1] Many of these assets will be either tax deferred and/or tax-free.

While this is a substantial figure—and it could generate a significant amount of wealth for many young savers—one of these types of accounts is a ticking time bomb. Why? Because the funds that will come from tax-deferred accounts will primarily be taxable upon withdrawal.

So how can young savers avoid having to hand over a sizable chunk of their inheritance to Uncle Sam?

One key strategy is for heirs not to take a lump sum when inheriting the money; however, nothing is that simple. And if you are the beneficiary of an IRA and you have no other income or savings, then taking the inheritance all at once may be your only choice.

## THE ROTH LEGACY: KEEP IT OVER LIFE EXPECTANCY

By this point in the book, if you have not yet discovered that tax-free is the best option, then we have probably failed in our tax-free rants. So we will reiterate here that the tax-free Roth option is the very best way to go.

In the case of inheriting assets, then, there is typically nothing better than a Roth option too. Let's take a look at an example. Say you inherit $100,000 in a Roth IRA. This account can be continued over your life expectancy. So, if you are forty years old at the time you inherit the funds, your life expectancy would be roughly thirty-eight more years.

If you then take out 2.5 percent each year from the Roth account, and the funds inside of it are still growing at a 10 percent rate of return, then you will still be attaining a 7.5 percent increase in the Roth account that is growing on a tax-free basis.

Alternatively, if you were to take all the money out of that Roth IRA and invest the funds into a nice dividend-paying portfolio, you would be required to pay tax on 100 percent of that gain each year.

In fact, any investment that you make with the funds after surrendering the Roth account would now be taxable for the next thirty-eight years. This can make a substantial difference over time in terms of how much you will actually keep.

## Estate taxes—don't worry

You may have heard or read about estate taxes, and how this type of tax can literally consume more than half of one's entire estate if not planned for properly. Let's set the record straight on estate taxes.

First, let us say that unless your parents have more than $10 million in assets, this is something that you will not have to worry about. If, however, they do have in excess of $10 million in assets, hopefully a nice chunk of this is invested in Roth options.

Individuals and couples who have $10 million, $20 million, or more should definitely talk with a qualified estate-tax expert.

Don't let your parents (or grandparents) be like Michael Jackson and have no plan. While Michael was a talented musician, he was not quite as talented when it came to planning for his estate and his beneficiaries.

Even Bill Gates has a plan to pay no estate tax to Uncle Sam by leaving his estate to his favorite charity. He learned this strategy from Warren Buffett, who wants to make sure that the US government does not get its hands on his $20 billion in the form of estate taxes.

## The traditional IRA: a ticking tax time bomb

While the inherited Roth IRA option will allow you to continue receiving your gains tax-free, inheriting a traditional IRA can be another story. In this case, if you inherit a traditional IRA that has, for instance, $100,000 in it, these funds will be 100 percent taxable to you as ordinary income.

So let's say that a young, forty-year-old couple who is in the 39.6 percent tax bracket inherits a traditional IRA with $100,000 in it. If they cash out in order to obtain the funds, then they would owe $39,600 to Uncle Sam, leaving only $60,400 to invest. And if they use that $60,400 to purchase dividend-paying stocks in a regular investment account, then they would also have to pay taxes on those gains for the rest of their lives.

Yes, these ticking-time-bomb funds can still be held inside of an inherited IRA, and the couple could opt to just make withdrawals from that account. But those payments coming out of the inherited traditional IRA would be taxable to them as income.

## THE BOTTOM LINE

The government is closely watching this $30 trillion in assets that will soon be heading to many young savers. And it is not surprising that the government has also introduced regulations that would require investment advisors to cut their fees on these funds. This is because the estimated share of fee savings alone is in the neighborhood of $17 billion per year.

These regulations, however, are not really designed to protect customers from the fees of investment advisors. So do not be fooled by the "customers come first" disguise. These regulations have much more to do with fees that could cut into the government's future tax revenue, because if Uncle Sam estimates an average 20 percent tax bracket on this $30 trillion, then almost $7 trillion would belong to the federal government.

With that in mind, remember that taking a lump sum of inherited assets can make the government your own biggest beneficiary. On the other hand, by leaving funds inside of Roth accounts, you can make the absolute most of this money both now and in the future.

1. Michael P. Regan, "Wall Street Has Its Eyes on Millennials' $30 Trillion Inheritance," *Bloomberg*, March 3, 2015, http://www.bloomberg.com/news/articles/2015-03-03/wall-street-has-its-eyes-on-millennials-30-trillion-inheritance. Accessed October 26, 2016.

CHAPTER 9

# Retirement Certainty with the Check-a-Month Plan

• • •

As we aim for retirement and we have saved a nice tax-free snowball, certainty in receiving income through retirement checks is a must. Social Security monthly checks are a real benefit that is certain for most retirees. These checks are essentially an annuity. Not only are these checks directly deposited into retirees' accounts, but they also come with the benefit of a generous government that promises that the checks will be increased based on inflation every year.

This is definitely too good to be true. But it is also coming from the government, and remember, this is the entity that also taxes Social Security benefits so that the wealthy pay more in taxes and in turn net less in their pockets.

### Finding certain income in retirement

Today, in the low-interest-rate environment and with virtually a 0 percent yield on money funds, certainty is not easy to find. For example, if you have $100,000 in a money fund and you want to get a check for $500 a month ($6,000 per year), the money fund with a 0 percent return will run out in sixteen years. That's because the money that is in the account isn't growing in order to replenish what you've been taking out of it.

On top of that, you might also be charged various fees from your bank, depending on the type of account you have. In this case, the account may run out of money in only fifteen years. So because you don't know how long you will live and need this income, neither the bank nor the money fund offers you certainty.

Instead of taking your money out of a money fund, though, what if a quality company would take your $100,000 and promise you a check for $470 per month ($5,640 per year)? The company would promise to pay you this $5,640 for twenty years, and if you are alive after twenty years, it will keep on paying.

Imagine if someone who is seventy years old deposited $100,000 into this quality company, and at age ninety-nine he is still getting $5,640 per year, providing him with a total payout of $163,560 over that twenty-nine-year period. In other words, lifetime payments! You can get this income certainty with an annuity.

Now, you may have heard a variety of information about annuities. For instance, there are some lawyers and money managers who hate annuities. However, the annuities that are offered through quality companies like TIAA, New York Life, and USAA Life can meet retirees' need for income certainty.

## Who uses annuities?

The reality is that we use annuities quite a lot. For example, the ongoing lifetime income that people receive from Social Security runs under the same premise as an annuity: certain income for life, no matter how long you live.

When lawyers complained to financial advisors about selling annuities, my mother purchased six of them. I personally use four annuities for my certainty in retirement. I receive lifetime income from my mother's annuities too in order to remind me of her and to spread the tax-deferred assets out over time.

## How annuities work to provide income

The term *annuity* simply means payout. The mathematical formula for an annuity would look as follows:

**Annuity Payment = Lump-Sum Deposit + Interest Earnings / Number of Years (time)**

Here are three simple examples of how a $100,000 lump-sum deposit into an annuity might pay out:

1) If, in our low-interest-rate climate (with money funds yielding 0 percent), you give one of the three quality companies mentioned above a $100,000 annuity deposit, they would pay out $6,000 per year for twenty years. This would give you a total payout of $120,000 over your lifetime. This means that the company gave you $20,000 in interest over the twenty-year time period, or $2,000 in interest per year.
2) If you instead ask the insurance company for lifetime payments with twenty years certain, then an annual payment would be closer to $5,800 per year. And if you live past the twenty years, the $5,800 would still be paid. In this case, income would be paid for at least twenty years. If you did

not live through that twenty-year time period, then the annuity's income would be paid out to a named beneficiary.
3) If you want to ensure that your spouse will also be able to receive lifetime income, you could choose to go with a joint and survivor payout. In this case, the annuity would pay out income for you and another person for as long as both people live. Here, the amount of the monthly or annual payment would be smaller than with just one income recipient. This is because the company is paying for the longer of two lifetimes.

## Will you have income certainty in retirement?

Now, we know that a lawyer or a money manager would not be able to pay out income for life with certainty. As we saw in the example above, the money fund could stop paying out in just sixteen years or even less when you factor in the fees that you might be hit with. And if you invest like Bernie Madoff, the payments might even stop in ten years!

The examples above are for fixed annuities. But there are other types of annuities available too. For instance, variable annuities have their return tied to equity investments such as mutual funds. With these types of annuities, you have the opportunity to get a higher return, but as with any other market-related entity, you also have greater risk.

Also, the examples above are for immediate annuities. That means that you would deposit a lump sum of money, and the annuity would begin paying out the income to you immediately, or at least within a very short time.

If you have several (or many) years before you retire, you could instead go with a deferred annuity. These annuities allow you to either deposit a lump sum or deposit money over time.

Today, in a deferred fixed annuity, you may be able to get a rate of just under 2 percent, which is much better than 0 percent with money funds or even 1.29 percent with five-year US bonds. And you are guaranteed to receive income for life when you need it in the future with the annuity.

Annuities can also be set up to pay out money for more than just one generation. So using a twenty- or thirty-year certain payout with a lifetime benefit with tax-free dollars can be a way to remember a parent or other loved one and to receive tax-free income every month.

Imagine Ken and Mary, the hypothetical couple that we referenced earlier in the book, taking a deposit of $1 million to a quality insurance company that would pay them $51,000 tax-free for the rest of both of their lifetimes and at least twenty years certain.

No lawyer or banker would ever even try to obtain that benefit for his clients because he knows it could not be done. Only the US government could accomplish this, and it would throw in an inflation increase every year.

Hopefully, young savers will get on the tax-free savings path early, as this can allow the ability to build a giant tax-free snowball that can be used for retirement income as well as for passing on a tax-free check to loved ones for their lifetimes too.

## SUMMARY / RULES FOR YOUNG SAVERS

• • •

1. Do not take a student loan without a way to pay it off.
   Example: Borrowing for a law degree is OK if you know you want to work for the federal government and will have the loan forgiven.
2. Avoid credit-card debt.
   Example: A $5,000 credit-card debt at 10 percent is way too high when the rate on most mortgages today is 4 percent. Anything above 4 percent is not going to help with building a snowball.
3. Save 10 percent of your income from every paycheck. If you can save 20 percent starting out, and your income grows, then your snowball will grow twice as fast.
4. Capitalism is good.
   Examples: Apple, Google, Facebook, Amazon.
5. A long-term investment horizon has proven to be successful. Plenty of good investment professionals can help you here.
6. Tax-free accounts must be used. The second-best type of account is tax deferred.
   Example: A back-door Roth IRA.
7. Demand that your employer offer Roth 401(k) accounts or a Roth 403(b).

8. Watch the amount in tax-deferred accounts that convert low capital gain rates and low dividend rates into ordinary income rates.
9. Diversifying your investments is good. Putting all of your eggs in one basket, however, can be dangerous.
10. With young families, term life insurance is the best type of tax-free protection for the cost.
11. College savings are best in a 529 plan.
12. Affluent young savers should look at variable universal life or dividend-paying whole life insurance.
13. Remember Rule 6 and be generous with a giving fund.
14. Work with a quality "client-first" financial company.
15. Work with a quality financial advisor who likes tax-free retirement savings alternatives.

Regardless of where you are starting from, it is never too early to start using tax-free options in order to help enhance your future retirement income. There are many ways that you could currently be sabotaging your retirement by following the "tried and true" investment advice that is preached by most financial advisors today.

If you closely follow the steps that are outlined in this book, you will have a running start towards growing assets over time, and in turn, having a larger well to draw from when the time comes to convert your savings into an ongoing income stream.

The bottom line: believe in future growth. Because when you invest using the most advantageous tax-free strategies, you are likely to reap some nice rewards down the road.

Footnote: There will be tax law changes, especially seven individual tax brackets being reduced to three or four brackets. However, our belief is that even if the percentage tax changes, tax revenue will not. Furthermore, tax-free compounding will still be very valuable.

RESOURCES

• • •

## Chapter 1
Debt.com: www.Debt.com
Consumer Credit Counseling Services: www.credit.org/cccs/
National Foundation for Credit Counseling: www.nfcc.org

## Chapter 2
www.IRS.gov

## Chapter 3
IRS guide to types of retirement plans: www.irs.gov/retirement-plans/plan-sponsor/types-of-retirement-plans-1
Roth IRAs: www.RothIRA.com

## Chapter 4
Social Security Administration: www.ssa.gov

## Chapter 5
Life insurance (Northwestern Mutual): www.lifeinsurance.com
Life insurance quotes: www.insure.com
Life insurance quotes: www.truebluelifeinsurance.com
A. M. Best Company: www.ambest.com
Standard & Poor's ratings criteria: www.standardandpoors.com/en_US/web/guest/ratings/ratings-criteria
Find ratings for top insurance companies: www.insure.com/interactive-tools/sandp/newtool1.jsp

## Chapter 6
529 plan information from the US Securities and Trade Commission: www.sec.gov/investor/pubs/intro529.htm
529 plan information from the IRS: www.irs.gov/uac/529-plans-questions-and-answers
Qualified tuition program information from the IRS: www.irs.gov/publications/p970/ch08.html

## Chapter 7
Life insurance:
Northwestern Mutual: www.lifeinsurance.com (160-year legacy)
New York Life: www.newyorklife.com (170-year legacy)

## Chapter 8
Benjamin F. Edwards & Company (125-year legacy)

**OTHER QUALITY COMPANIES:**
USAA: www.USAA.com (ninety-year legacy)
TIAA-CREF: www.TIAA-CREF.org (one-hundred-year legacy)

ABOUT THE AUTHORS

• • •

# Meade Greenberg and Tom Guignon

Tom Guignon is a forty-plus-year veteran of the financial-services industry. A 1967 graduate of West Point, Tom served in

Vietnam with the Fifth Special Forces until 1969. Because of his military background, Tom became a policyholder of the United Services Automobile Association (USAA) and has been a proud surplus owner of USAA for nearly fifty years.

In 1971, Tom joined Bache as an investment broker and four years later moved to A. G. Edwards, a true "client comes first" company. Throughout his time there, Tom played a key role in starting the financial planning department—which eventually became the managed products department—and grew the area from a team of just five individuals to more than one hundred.

His department handled mutual funds, annuities, insurance, limited partnerships, alternative investments, unit trusts, commodity funds, mutual fund advisory programs, and individually managed accounts. These managed products accounted for over 60 percent of A. G. Edwards's revenues when, in 2008, Wachovia purchased the company, and within less than one year, it was bought by Wells Fargo. Tom remained with the firm until his retirement in 2011.

That same year, Tom helped with the start-up of Benjamin F. Edwards & Company, an investment firm that puts the client first. Today, he serves as an author and a full-time consultant on tax-free financial planning. Tom resides in St. Louis, Missouri, with his wife, Emily.

## Meade Greenberg

Meade Guignon Greenberg is a middle-school math teacher. She was born and raised in St. Louis, Missouri, absorbing her father's rants about the beauty of tax-free planning. Meade earned her undergraduate degree in economics from the University of Michigan.

After a year in the real world, she decided that working with children was preferable to working with adults. Meade has now been teaching for ten years, and she lives with her husband in San Francisco.

www.ingramcontent.com/pod-product-compliance
Lightning Source LLC
Chambersburg PA
CBHW060359190526
45169CB00002B/660